A Social History of the Fool

A Social History of the Fool

SANDRA BILLINGTON

Lecturer in Renaissance Drama
University of Glasgow

THE HARVESTER PRESS · SUSSEX
ST. MARTIN'S PRESS · NEW YORK

First published in Great Britain in 1984 by
THE HARVESTER PRESS LIMITED
Publisher: John Spiers
16 Ship Street, Brighton, Sussex

and in the USA by
ST. MARTIN'S PRESS, INC.
175 Fifth Avenue, New York, N.Y. 10010

British Library Cataloguing in Publication Data

Billington, Sandra
    A social history of the fool.
    1. Fools and jesters
    I. Title.

    398'.042   GT3670

    ISBN 0-7108-0610-8

Library of Congress Cataloging in Publication Data

Billington, Sandra
    A social history of the fool

    Bibliography: p.
    Includes index.
    1. Fools and jesters–England–History. 2. Fools
and jesters in literature. I. Title.
GT3670. B45   1984   306'.48   83-40624
ISBN 0-312-73293-7 (U.S.)

Typeset in 11pt Baskerville by
P.R.G. Graphics Limited, Redhill, Surrey
Printed in Great Britain by
Butler & Tanner Ltd, Frome, Somerset

Contents

List of Abbreviations

E.E.T.S.
Early English Text Society
J.E.F.D. & S.S.
Journal of the English Folk Dance and Song Society
P.M.L.A.
Publications of the Modern Language Association of America
P.Q.
Philological Quarterly
S.P.
Studies in Philology

Introduction

It may seem impertinent to say this, but the Fool in English society has so far only received a very limited amount of attention despite the excellent work of Enid Welsford and others. The reason is that the Fool has always been regarded as a temporary fashion in England (imported from the continent) and his dates rarely cross the boundaries of 1500 to 1600. In a way this is hardly surprising since many of the Fool's literate peers hoped that he would indeed be only a temporary fashion and in the Middle Ages in particular they simply ignored what they could not stop. And so it was only in the sixteenth century, when Fools became popular, that literature and records included extensive information about them. After about 1620 anathema returned and official records attempted to give the impression that Fools and Fool-games had been eliminated from society. However, the Fools went back to their low-life roots and survived there with considerable tenacity and financial reward until the early nineteenth century. Charles Hardwick wrote from Manchester in 1872 about Fools and their seasonal games and said that even the most severe threats failed to frighten them 'out of the heart of the mass of the population and they survive to the present day' (p. 59).

I must apologise though for the meandering path of the character. The beginning goes back to the Middle Ages and Fool customs at this period have never been assessed before, therefore it's essential to include the early period and I ask for the patience of the non-specialist reader, who may find this period a little distant. The second apparent digression comes during the eighteenth century, when there was a change by some from Fool status to that of the respectable comedian. And at the same time Harlequin and then the clown filled the gap. And finally, there was the unbroken source of ideas to be drawn on in the fairgrounds, where professionals and seasonal players mixed. The fairground acted as a vast catchment area for local people to imitate the professionals and sometimes to influence them. Shortened versions of high-society London plays were presented—frequently grotesquely—as Drolls. Circuses performed in the country and a variety of other travelling shows arrived, including the mountebank and his comic servant, who was, of course, a descendant of the Elizabethan Fool. As Sybil Rosenfeld says of the theatre in the London fairs, popular taste was conservative, 'clinging to the old tales. Secondly, it demanded the ancient relief of comic interlude, revelling in swiftly alternating contrasts of marvellous feats and knockabout farce, fustian and slapstick. Thirdly, it required an admixture of singing and dancing, so that all the elements of the Elizabethan jig (which was Fool entertainment) survived in the booths to entertain the descendents of the Elizabethan groundlings' (p. 149). Had it not been for the fairs, the Fool might not have kept his freedom for so long and it is also possible that the textual versions of mumming plays might not have developed as they did. And so we find that the walks of life of the Fool are like the roots of the buttercup and crop up where least expected to inspire or infect the thinking of several centuries, depending on one's reaction to him. However, it is true that the fairground Fool was used as a satirical mouthpiece and butt for eighteenth-century political pamphleteers.

Where authors are listed in the bibliography I have given page references in the text only. Other quotations are explained in footnotes. Finally, I would like to express my gratitude to the British Academy and to Glasgow University for financial help towards the research; and to all those people whose interest has stimulated a constant supply of anecdotes and helpful suggestions.

CHAPTER 1

The existence of the Fool in medieval England

It appears that in England in the Middle Ages the word 'fool' was more than the abstract term of abuse which it appears to be today, but placed the owner of the name within a recognizable relation to a figure in cap and bell. At the same period in France such an association was clearer for a man called *sot*; however, in England such was not the case. Two of the most famous early Fools were not called Fool at all. Hitard, jester to the Saxon King Edmund Ironside was called *joculator* and Rahere, of Henry I's twelfth-century court, was referred to as a minstrel. Both were greatly rewarded by their patrons and enjoyed a degree of independence not to be known again by English Fools until the sixteenth century. It is interesting that both men felt called to end their lives in pilgrimage to Rome and each willed significant religious bequests. Hitard left Walworth to Canterbury and Rahere founded St Bartholomew's Hospital.[1] Appropriately, therefore, the famous fair which was the great annual event at St Bartholomew's and which was to be the Fool's refuge for the next seven centuries, was itself founded by a Fool. In the words of a nineteenth-century antiquarian, 'Gentlemen, on this anniversary of St. Bartholomew, let us not forget that we owe this Fair to a priest and jester': (Daniel, p. 201).

However, at first sight, the medieval English countryside was devoid of colourful figures in cap and bell, who in France led Carnival entertainments and imposed a period of disorder as welcome to the people as unwelcome to the authorities. Sir Edmund Kirchever Chambers in his fine work on medieval drama appeared to have found the reason why. The ecclesiastic Feast of Fools was totally subdued in England by the end of the fourteenth century, whereas in France, despite decrees, protests and impositions, the lower clergy continued to indulge their annual usurped authority until the sixteenth century. Since secular Fool activity in France also developed into societies and scripted *sot* plays, it was assumed that the early demise of the church feast in England prevented similar emulation, and consequently, popular cap and bell activity never had chance to take root. However, it is now known that church and secular customs existed apart from each other, even though they doubtlessly had aspects in common.[2] As far as French Fool societies are concerned, Natalie Zeman Davis writes that secular societies 'existed in some form in French cities from the thirteenth century on, contemporaneous with the cathedral *fête*'.[3] The importance of this with regard to English social behaviour is that we can consider on its own merits fragmented evidence which had previously not been looked for or, when seen, appeared as unimportant anomalies. The fragmentation is partly accounted for by Richard Axton's observation that 'the Church's virtual monopoly of written records and its concern with conserving the Word, led to rather full documentation of its own traditional Latin drama'.[4] Further, lack of comment now seems tacit disapproval rather than rarity of occurrence, for even prior to the extirpation of the church's own *regis stultorum* (Feast of Fools) only one solitary comment on Fools in society appears. This is found in a neglected passage of the *Summa Confessorum*, written by Thomas of Chobham about 1220. He wrote:

> It is known that until now there has been the perverse custom in many places, where on any holy feast day wanton women and youthful fools gather together and sing wanton and diabolical songs the whole night through in the churchyards and in the church to which they lead their ring dances and practise many other shameful games. All such activity is to be prohibited with the greatest diligence, if it is possible. However, it is encouraged in many places for many men would not otherwise come to such feasts if they could not play games.[5]

Chobham is disarming in his honesty over the pragmatism of many of his brethren and the account of social disturbances in churches complements records of liberties taken in the sixteenth century. For when, in 1535—a year before official restraint was placed on holy day games—the youths of the parish of Harwich entered the church on St Stephen's Day, led by a piper, to choose them 'A Lord of Misrule, as has been the custom in years past', the vicar, Thomas Colthorpe, broke the pipe over the player's head and, it was claimed, caused a general disturbance.[6] Chobham acknowledged that such occurrence was habitual, even indigenous before his time; therefore one cannot attribute his lone thirteenth-century comment to the occasional eruption. Further information to be included here leads to the same conclusion. Fool behaviour was largely suffered in silence as it couldn't be prevented.

It is worth looking again at Chambers' examples of the church feast evidenced in England at Lincoln and Beverley. In both cases one finds reference to a separate secular custom. The 1398 Statutes concerning the better government of the church at Beverley are uncompromising over the extirpation of the corrupt church custom of *regis stultorum* at New Year.[7] However, the Statutes continue (and this Chambers omits) that the ancient church custom in Beverley called *les Fulles* will continue. What this might have involved is indicated in visual rather than written evidence. In the church are carvings of Fools. The earliest (*c* 1330) depicts a grotesque: a crouching figure 'half human, half animal, with hooves and an animal's legs, but wearing a two-eared cap of a fool on a grotesque human face'.[8] Four other carvings of men wearing cap and bell are found on the later misericords of about 1520. Since, in the Statutes of 1398, approval for *les Fulles* is incorporated among permissable Christmas games for the laity, it would seem that the Christmas season was where the feast belonged in the Church Calendar.

At Lincoln, after Archbishop Grosseteste forbade the ecclesiastic feast in 1236, William Courtney intervened a century and a half later, when he found that the vicars 'were still in the habit of disturbing divine service on January 1st, in the name of the Feast' (Chambers,[9] vol. 1, p. 322). This is the final reference to the church feast in England and since it occurs at almost the same date as the reforms carried out at Beverley, Chambers concludes that from the end of the fourteenth century English vicars were probably obliged to forgo their New Year privileges. However, he adds the word 'probably' in relation to a fifteenth-century reference to feasting in Lincoln. This took place in *ultimo natali*, the last day of Christmas or the Epiphany. Chambers wrote: 'what was ly ffolcfeste of which Canon John Marshall complained in Bishop Alnwick's visitation of 1437 that he was called upon to bear the expense?' (p. 322, note). *Ly ffolcefeste* is an Anglo-French name like the name of the Beverley feast and, although Canon Marshall questioned its propriety, he nevertheless promised to maintain it at his own expense,[10] which means that this celebration would have continued further into the fifteenth century. Since no further reference is found to the *regis stultorum*—the name of the church feast— one can only conclude that surviving feasts were secular and, like the games suffered to be played in churches, were permitted in preference to the abstention of the entire congregation.

The end of the fourteenth century saw a watershed in ecclesiastical definitions of the Fool and the theology is explored in Chapter 2. For, despite growing disapproval from church and court written evidence can be found for the activities of Fools over this period and coincidental with the change in church attitudes, it appears that Fool behaviour also underwent a change. Evidence from the earlier half of the fourteenth century shows that Fool games involved stripping oneself naked, possibly in imitation of the real idiot. In Exeter College, Oxford, is an *Etymology* of about 1300 in which the definition of *cachinor* is accompanied by a prancing figure, naked save for the two-eared hood, bauble, ornamental sword (which was to become the hallmark of the Fool in drama) and, curiously, a single shoe. The definition of *cachinor* is given as one who from ancient times is said to laugh immoderately and without intelligence.[11] The definition could cover the idiot or the idiot's mimic and no strong condemnation is implied apart from the degrading aspects of such behaviour. However, theology is a vital aspect in assessing social values regarding the Fool and two of the main iconographical sources of evidence are Psalters and Bibles. Before 1350 illuminations accompanying the Psalm beginning 'The fool hath said in his heart there is no God'[12] consistently show a naked or semi-naked figure with bauble and occasionally a bell on his eared hood. The group of English Psalters of this period which repeatedly use this motif, albeit with variations in iconographical meaning, are the Peterborough Psalters.[13] Others show a roughly-clad man carrying a phallic-shaped bauble.[14]

These pictures complement written evidence. As I have said, ecclesiastic and popular customs could have elements in common and one distinct factor which pre-1350 Fools of church and laity both had was this curious indulgence of returning to the natural state. In about 1280 the French theologian, Guilelmus Peraldus, wrote a scientifically detailed study of the Vices and Virtues. One of his conclusions was that every sin had two forms: an inner and an outer; and Pride, the greatest sin, carried two outer manifestations. One was self-decoration and the other self-denudation and Peraldus uses Fools as examples of men who betray themselves by both manifestations. Firstly, he condemns men who beg ornaments with which to decorate themselves. Secondly, he attacks the opposite amusement indulged in by both the clerics at the Feast of Fools and men from other sections of society. The examples he takes are

those that believe themselves well clothed and decorated, in the way that the body of their horses are well clothed, to the extent that they all go naked. [These] are like a certain kind of cleric who, at the Feast of Fools, puts his horse in scarlet and himself puts on rushes.[15]

The example is in keeping with the purpose of the Feast of Fools, which was that of inversion—'putting down the mighty from their seats and exalting the humble and meek'. By a logical extension the horse is given clerical red and the cleric puts on the horse's saddle. A splendid secular example is given by Constance Bullock-Davies in her study of the London Whitsuntide celebrations of 1306. In the records are payments made to those within the court and to those who had come from outside to entertain the King. Since Davies concludes that more details were kept about outsiders, it would appear that the following onslaught came from the environs of London: 'To Bernard, the Fool, and 54 of his companions coming naked before the King, with dancing revelry'.[16] This group visited twice and their behaviour was clearly not thought indecent or abnormal.

However, by 1380 the decorated Fool was predominant. Other customs such as leaping naked over Midsummer bonfires continued well into the sixteenth century, but there is no indication that these men were Fools, although attempts were made to discourage them. And the later record of certain gentry in the time of Charles II causing disturbance in London by cavorting naked in the streets gives no indication that they were virtuously preserving a tradition. Instead, by 1380, fine portraits of decorated Fools appear in English Psalters. (For a fairly complete list see Appendix.) One of the most striking illustrations comes from the Richard II Bible, where the Fool's evil influence on society is graphically shown. In this painting the left hand side shows a group of men and women, laughing, talking and embracing. Despite this behaviour appearing a normal depiction of society, the Fool who watches on the right has a finger to his lips and points warningly to the heavens, where God looks down in distress, not at the crowd, but at the Fool. And to reinforce the satanic implications of the Fool, the man does not lift up his eyes to heaven while pointing. The meaning appears to be that earthly folly is embodied in the Fool, who wishes it to escape the notice of God. In nearly all the illustrations where the artist intended a moral message, the detail of reproof and guilt is varied so that each illumination has an individual idea behind it. But one other early clothed Fool illustrating Psalm 13 or 52 (the Psalm was repeated in these early Psalters) shows not only the artist's talent but also secular delight in his work. The illustration comes from Corpus Christi College, Oxford, MS (E)18: fol. 44v and contains a Fool in the complete costume of pointed, belled hood, close-fitting tunic and hose, all centrally divided into red and white halves. The Fool rides a hobby horse and carries a thonged whip. Behind him is a stream with a wooden bridge and he looks down at a blossoming bush. Were it not for the context of the Psalm, one could take this miniature as a celebration of summer and the outdoor freedom of the season. However, the date was about 1380 and whatever the artist's personal views, the illustration has to be seen as intended condemnation of the Fool in his now decorated ostentation. This change from the Peterborough tradition of the first half of the century is marked almost beyond recognition. Whereas Lucy Freeman Sandler's examples consistently reveal a shaven, naked figure, illuminations after 1350 turn to one totally covered by hood, tunic and hose. There is, however, an important point of contrast between written evidence and illuminations. Pictures of Fools are usually set in a summer landscape, whereas comments on Fools set them among winter games.

Chaucer provides an unexpected example. Cavorting Fools and a Fool-grotesque are woven into the narrative of his *Hous of Fame,* written about 1384. The time of year is exact: ' . . . of Decembre the tenthe day' [Book 1, line 111]. According to pre-Reformation Calendars, this was two days after the Feast of our Lady and three before St Lucy's Day. As the poem is written in three books, Chaucer may well have intended the last and wryly doom-ridden book to coincide with St Lucy's Day— the shortest day of the year. However, once the poem begins all sense of natural season disappears for Chaucer draws attention to inanimate features, and it appears that it is the behaviour of the people rather than the season which is paramount. Such a view corresponds with the comment made over a century earlier when Chobham said that the games Chaucer dwells on in Book 3 could take place on any holy day of the year, regardless of season. To cancel out specific season, Chaucer describes the mountain, where the House or Castle stands as a 'rock of ice', the Castle 'of stone of Beryl' and the Lady herself a grotesque, very like the early Beverley carving. She is part bird, part animal and part human, and among these attractions are 'many long ears', which inevitably connect her with asinine behaviour. In Book 1, Chaucer is introduced under his own name, Geoffrey, musing on classical themes of infidelity in love for his poetic inspiration. He is abruptly interrupted by an eagle, with feathers of gold, who lifts Geoffrey by the scruff of the neck and lectures him on his lack of real knowledge. The poet is faithful to the romantic muse but has no personal experience. The eagle points out that Geoffrey always writes of distant lands and ancient times but

> . . . of thy verray neyghebores
> That duellen almost at thy dores,
> Thou herist neyther that ne this.   [lines 649-51]

To complete his education, therefore, Geoffrey is taken to witness the wooing behaviour and other pastimes of his own land and in Book 3 is set down at the foot of the mountain to learn for himself. There is a reference to 'alleskinnes condiciouns/That dwelle in erthe under the mone', yet Geoffrey the poet as well as Geoffrey the narrator would have been equally ignorant of ancient times and it would seem that the games he watches throughout Book 3 were taken from Chaucer's real knowledge of social activities in England and about which he is usually silent. Firstly, there are details of minstrels and story tellers, harp-players and other musicians, including the harvest-home piper. Geoffrey notices with surprise that famous people are learning 'love-daunces, springes/Reyes, and these straunge thinges' and here there seems to be the indication that in the peaceful years before civil war between Richard II and Boling-broke, country dances were becoming popular at court. Geoffrey watches the tricks of jugglers, magicians and other entertainers, called tregetours, who practise sleight-of-hand. All these forms of entertainment are depicted in the marginal illustrations of the fourteenth-century manuscript called *The Romance of Alexander* and are reproduced in Strutt's nineteenth-century work on *Sports and pastimes of the people of England*. (Interestingly, all the forms of display were to survive later in the fairgrounds, where the eye of authority could be evaded.) After a colourful description of the collection of sports, Geoffrey observes the reaction of all mankind when Lady Fame calls them to her. They flock before her and plead their suits. Man-kind divides into seven groups and the innocent poet assumes all to have equal right to justice; yet Lady Fame's responses are persistently arbitrary. She determines to 'trumpe al the contraire/Of they that han don well or faire [Book 3, 539-40]', but to some 'gode folk' she grants their 'gode werke be wist', to others, not; and those who pray for obscurity, saying that any good deeds were done for love of God, Lady Fame considers insane and insists on their high renown.

The suitors culminate in a wild group of men, who cavort, turn somersaults and shout so that the hall resounds:

> Tho come ther leapynge in a route,
> And gunne choppen al aboute

Every man upon the crowne,
That al the halle gan to sowne.   [1823-6]

They claim to be knaves who earn their living by their wicked-
ness; therefore, rather than have this concealed, they ask for
their 'fame' to be known in accordance with their characters.
After agreeing, Lady Fame asks:

But what art thou that seyst this tale,
That werest on thy hose a pale,
And on thy tipet such a belle?   [1839-41]

The editor, F. N. Robinson, notes 'pale—stripe. He wore the
garb of a fool' [p. 787]. Therefore, without even mentioning
'fool', Chaucer identifies a seventh part of humanity as those
who indulge in Fool behaviour and at least one of them, the
leader, is dressed in a belled cap and simple, parti-coloured
hose. The dress is not the elaborate one of a court jester but one
which an ordinary peasant might afford. From the description it
appears that a Fools' dance, such as that depicted in *The
Romance of Alexander*, or a Fool-led dance was a form of activity
which represented to Chaucer a seventh part of human activity.
Chaucer makes clear that, to him, it represents the nadir of
human behaviour. The trumpet proclamation of the knaves or
'shrewes' is the trump of doom and, when asked, Geoffrey
denies he has come to take part. The late fourteenth century
was the time when Churchmen like Courtney were attempting
reforms, so it could be argued that it is not surprising if writers
such as Chaucer made a passing, derogatory reference to the
custom. However, it can equally be argued that if it made up as
large a part of group activity as Chaucer says, then it is surprising that other fourteenth-century writers such as Gower
and Langland did not also include it; and the paucity of information in both the fourteenth and fifteenth centuries is not
necessarily evidence for or against its prevalence. Lack of comment is better explained as a choice to ignore what could not be
controlled. As Chobham said earlier, churchmen were
impotent to eradicate seasonal Fool behaviour and respectable
writers rarely demeaned themselves by reference to it. For
example, the attitude of the fifteenth-century churchman and

writer, Dan Lydgate, (who wrote after church prohibition of clerical games) is similar to that of Chaucer. Firstly, in his 'Order of Fools' in which the clergy themselves are the real subject of attack—ravening the sheep they should be protecting —the two kinds of social Fool, the idiot and the seasonal Fool, are included without stigma. The idiot is the man with 'face unstable, gasing East and South/with loud bursts of laughter he interrupts his speech/He gapes like a rook, with jaw wide open/Like a captured Jay enclosed in his cage'.[17] The rowdy Fool is a dancer who leads local entertainment: 'The tenth Fool may hop upon the ring/Foot pointed before him and lead the dance properly'.[18] A more subtle incorporation of this country, dancing Fool is found in one of Lydgate's Prologues to the courtly version of mumming. Lydgate is famous for the refinement he gave to mumming and all that remain are the Prologues, therefore it is possible that the performance proper was silent. Lydgate's themes are usually courtly and based on classical literature, yet in contrast to these is one written for the mumming at Hertford during Henry VI's winter celebrations of 1430. The introduction is in the form of an apology to the King for the low subject matter which, Lydgate explains, he would not have used except that a loyal countryman, now slain, had asked for it before leaving for France. The subject is 'a disguising of the rude country people complaining about their wives' and the action 'the perennial conflict between husband and wife for command in the home' (Wickham, p. 197). Folk games such as 'playing at the staff' are used as comic metaphor for the bullying treatment the men receive from their spouses. In conclusion their spokesman says:

> It is no game with wives for to play
> But for Fools

and such

> with his three-stringed fiddle may sing full often alas!
> And with these men here standing one by one
> He may with them go off to the dance
> here the narrator points to six rustics.[19]

Were it not for the physical presence of six countrymen standing there, like Chaucer's dancers who speak of standing in a
row, it would be easy to see the word 'foolis' in the first quota-
tion as metaphor only. However, behind the metaphor was the
reality of men's country dance and Fool behaviour, and which
can be seen to have had certain affinities with the sixteenth-
century Morris.[20] After the numerous wars began at the turn of
the fifteenth century, the courtly emphasis in entertainment
was on dignity and grace: all the aspects which had no violent
actions in them. The mumming at Hertford was an exception to
the rule which lasted until the peaceful reign of Henry VII
(1485). However, illustrations in *Psalters* still used the Fool to
illustrate Psalm 13 though some of them were later defaced.

A superb and complementary example of social Fool behaviour at this time occurs in a Scots poem called 'Cockelbie
Sow'. In this three-part romp there is no question of muted
disapproval by the author, nor detached irony. Rather, the
poem is full of vigorous enthusiasm. Its date is thought to be
fifteenth century, though it now survives in the Bannatyne
manuscript of 1568. In Part 3 we find a burlesque concerning a
recalcitrant pig and explicit Fool-led mayhem. The pig belong-
ing to the swineherds escapes its conversion to pork and causes
a chase. Eventually on the heath the swineherds meet with two
other groups of men: cowmen and shepherds and all three
dance. The text reads:

> Than all Assemblit wt a gamyn
> And all the menstralis attonis
> blew vp and playit for the nonis
> Schiphird nolt hirdis
> And suynhirdis out girdis
> ffor to dance merily
>
> A maister swynhird swanky
> And his cousing copyn cull
> ffowll of bellis fulfull
> led the dance and began.[21]

The clearest reading of the last four lines would appear to be: 'A
master swineherd, Swanky, and his cousin, Copyn Cull, a Fool
full of bells, led the dance and began'. Translations made so far

do not suggest this, preferring instead the possibility that the dancers had full bellies.[22] However, apart from more subtle arguments, the fact remains that the animal intended for this purpose remains very much alive. Bearing in mind English evidence, the Fool-led dance seems certain.

To complete the fundamental evidence that Fools were a part of the rural countryside in Britain throughout the Middle Ages and were not a sixteenth-century French import, I return to illustrations. As I have said there are numerous miniatures by English painters which use Fools for Psalter iconography; and since no explanation is given, the image chosen must have been one immediately recognizable to the reader. In France one finds some illustrations of Friars' or tonsured Fools. There is occasionally, as in MS Bodley 953, a gossiping Fool; a fashionable Fool in Trinity College, Cambridge MS 0.3.10; a Fool with blackened face in MS Bodley Liturg. 153 and frequently, a court jester with a King. The individual meanings conveyed by the Fool and King are numerous. Sometimes the King is admonishing the Fool, sometimes it is the Fool who accuses the King and in the British Library MS Royal 2.A.xii, the King and Fool mutually accuse each other. King and Fool disputes were common, the most famous being the various Solomon and Marcolf debates, in which Marcolf turns Solomon's wisdom to foolishness.[23] It was a popular joke to say that the state of King and Fool were the only ones to which you had to be born and could not otherwise attain, and Kings and the nobility frequently kept simpleton Fools to remind themselves of their own mortality and imperfections. The church in Western Europe encouraged this practice and the moral implications seem to have been realised more strongly in Britain than elsewhere. For example, the favourite story of a King turned Fool, *King Robert of Sicily,* had variants throughout Europe, which are compared by L.M. Hornstein. Whereas in the German version, the King is deposed while bathing, and the account of his struggle for recognition as King and not an idiot claiming to be King contains a simple delight in ridicule, the English version has Robert deposed by the angel while vaunting indomitable power in church. The season is Christmas and so the story uses the old church custom that at this time the Lord puts down the mighty from their seats. The angel takes Robert's place and the King's claims are taken to be the ravings of a madman, for which he is shaven and made to live as the angel's Fool until the King acknowledges God as his master and himself a Fool in comparison. The English version was made into a play and was performed until the early sixteenth century.

This interesting area takes us into the realm of court Fools and to further establish the existence of Fools outside the courts I have chosen three manuscript pictures in which the Fools cannot be mistaken for court jesters. The first is from the Wingfield Psalter and was executed in 1450 for the Stafford family. The delicacy of the borders suggests that the artist worked in the style and spirit of French and Flemish artists, but the delineation of the main figure follows English tradition. O.E. Saunders writes, 'the Wingfield Psalter . . . seems to show influence from France, especially in the borders, but the figures are of a heavy build not found in French manuscripts. The book was decorated in 1450, and is thus one of the latest good examples of English miniature painting'. [vol. 1, p. 118]. The heavy build of the central figure shows in the strain of the leg muscles, the breadth of shoulder and the broad, unrefined facial features. His dress consists of the parti-coloured hose and peaked shoes which the cleric, John Mirc, deplored.[24] Further, this Fool wears every accoutrement of his profession: bauble, thonged whip, bells in every conceivable place and a hood which combines long ears with a ribbed, pointed cap. In Leslie Hotson's interesting compilation of information, *Shakespeare's motley*, the hood is dismissed as Fool's headgear in favour of a detachable cap. 'We still speak of the fool's cap and bells, and of foolscap paper. What reason have we to imagine that Shake-spearean stage fools should wear hoods?' (p. 5). Despite references brought in to support this, it would appear that the issue is one of a change in nineteenth-century terminology and, possibly, a change of headwear at that date. In the early illustrations the headpiece is a combination of peaked cap (tippet or liripipe) and eared hood.[25] There is of course a practical reason. Since the Fool was noted for his highly ener-getic behaviour, the basic emblem of his profession would not otherwise long remain with him. In the Wingfield Psalter, the central Fool clearly wears a hood and his costume is both elaborate and well-fitting. Such would be beyond the means of a feudal peasant and this figure is probably a representation of a professional, household jester: perhaps the Stafford family Fool, although his origins may have been peasant. The drawing which makes this fine illustration so valuable is a less remarkable picture in the margin. Here, there is a humbly-dressed Fool swinging among the foliage. Again his face is rough and his dress corresponds exactly with that indicated by Chaucer almost a century earlier. He wears a hood with a bell on the tippet and his hose are decorated by a single stripe up the side. His sporting among the trees links this peasant Fool with that of the second picture, which brings us closer to the sixteenth century.

The illumination appears on a *Magna Carta,* written about 1495, which introduces a collection of Statutes from the reign of King John to that of Henry VII. The first initial, E, sports a Fool in saffron coat and hood perched on the middle bar of the letter. The coat extends into a tail with a bell on the end[26] and the tippet and sleeves also have bells. The costume follows precisely the design of that in the Richard II Bible a century earlier. In the belt of the *Magna Carta* Fool is a wooden ladle and the man feeds a squirrel from a wooden bowl. The association with rural England is unmistakable. Like the Wingfield Fools, his face is broad and unrefined, he is surrounded by foliage and at his feet sit two admiring dogs. Other marginalia include a shrewish wife, raising broom and flail in the threatening manner proclaimed by Lydgate. Supposing the decoration to have been influenced by Henry's peaceful accession, the meaning suggests the basic liberty of the people after the stringencies of war. If, however, the figures are purely means of decorating the page, they show that the illustrator was familiar with an English tradition concerning the dress and behaviour of rural Fools.

The final example, about 1520, is a delightful exception to the rule that the literate, particularly clerics, eschewed Fool indulgence. The document is a fragementary copy of Statutes of St John's College, Cambridge. Initial letters have been decorated with portraits of men in Fools' caps and, in other cases, sober-faced men are mocked by Fools. Understandably, this copy was not that finally adopted by the College. However, the visual licence coincides with other evidence that Fool drama was known in the College almost from the date of its foundation.[27]

In conclusion, one can see that the accumulation of oblique references and tacit disapproval mounts to the level where one can say Fool behaviour was seen as an inevitable part of medieval life and that the literati tried to turn a blind eye to it. There is a curious discrepancy between the written references, which speak of winter activity, and the pictures of summer Fools. The most cogent reasons seem to be that (a) since ecclesiastic documents include the mention of secular behaviour in relation to the church's banned feast, that reference would have to be a winter one. (b) it is known that the court and universities usually received outside entertainers at Christmas when they too were enjoying a period of general celebration. The fact that the Whitsuntide court of Edward I includes a record of visiting Fools shows how dependent we are on court and church records. Their scarce references are the clues we have of the behaviour of the largely illiterate population. For example, warmer weather would release men inclined to Fool games from dependence on indoor shelter and, therefore, without the rare court appearance there might have been no written account of them at all. One returns to Chobham's comment that the people's games could erupt on any holy day in the Middle Ages, if opportunity afforded. Seasons such as Lent broke up the times into winter and summer periods, and since the participants were illiterate, unlike the French *sots*, they had no means of leaving their own record or of expressing their own point of view of society.

CHAPTER 2

Theological and philosophical attitudes to the Fool

When Chaucer's Fools claimed to be full of vice and wicked habits, for which they wanted to be renowned, Chaucer was following mainstream theological opinion about Fools in England in his time. However, there is a paradox to bear in mind. At the base of Christian belief is St Paul's teaching, and fundamental to this is that the Christian is a Fool in the eyes of the world, 'because that which is foolishness to God is wisdom to men, and what is weakness to God is strength to men'.[1] St Paul associates himself and his companions with the social Fool of the East. In 1 Corinthians 4; verses 9 and 10 he wrote: 'For I think that God has exhibited the apostles as the lowest creatures, as it were intended for death. For we are made a spectacle to the world: both to angels and to men. We are fools for Christ's sake'.[2] As Enid Welsford has shown, eastern Fools were mystics or semi-mystics, who diverted society by their unworldliness, but nevertheless were also respected for it (p. 56), and the later Latin translations of the Greek Bible retained *stultus* for St Paul's letter, though the Psalm usually illustrated with a Fool was modified to read *'dixit insipiens in corde suo: non est Deus'*. *Insipiens* includes all unwise men, whereas *stultus* more often referred to the man who was the recognizable figure in society. At first sight, St Paul's writing conflicts with later western theology and the confusion arises from the use of one word for 'fool' in western languages, where Hebrew had and still has two. One, *tam*, means the innocent Fool, who has no regard for material rewards. The other comes from the root, *ksl*, and contains the wilful, evil meanings of folly. Thus the Psalm, which in English Psalters used the icon of the social Fool, means the second; and St Paul meant the first. 'The mode of [St Paul's] thinking is Hebrew-Aramaic; it arouses positive and pleasant associations of completeness and integrity'.[4] Present-day

Yiddish retains the distinction. Isaac Bashevis-Singer's famous story, *Gimpel the Fool,* is called *Gimpel Tam* and begins *'Ikh bin Gimpel Tam. Ikh halt mikh nisht far keyn nar.*[3] *Farkert.*[4] In English this reads: 'I am Gimpel the fool. I don't think myself a fool. On the contrary'. Not only is the original distinction lost but there arises a familiar contradiction. The fool who thinks he is not a fool is an even greater fool. And so the original meaning is inverted.

As western Europe became Christianised 'fool' initially retained St Paul's meaning and meant the witless man. The two early English court jesters were not known by anything other than *joculator* and minstrel. The closeness of the witless man to God was stressed, since the innocence of the natural had links with Christian or Pauline folly. The late Anglo-Saxon translation of Pope Gregory's *Pastoral Care* reads:

> It is not necessary to advise the simple to forsake their wiles, for they have them not. Therefore, it is much easier for them to rise to righteous wisdom ... About the same thing St. Paul spoke: 'Whoever among you thinks himself the wisest in guiles, let him first become foolish, that he may thence become wise.   [pp. 202-05]

Until the meaning of 'natural Fool' changed in the sixteenth century, the innocence of the natural remained in church teaching and the innocent folly of the Christian was central to monastic tradition.[5] Further, Christian folly was not wholly omitted from the Liturgy, nor from early religious plays. Firstly, St Paul's second letter to the Corinthians, verses 19-23, was read as the Epistle for the Sunday prior to Shrovetide: Sexagesima Sunday. The first official translation reads:

> Ye suffre fooles gladly, seying ye yourselves are wise. For ye suffre if a man bring you into bondage: yf a man deuoure: yf a man take: if a man exalte himselfe: if a man smite you on the face. I speak as concernyng rebuke, as though we had been weake in this behalfe. Howbeit, whereinsoeuer any man dare be bold (I speak folishly) I dare be bold also. They are Hebrues, even so am I. They are Israelytes, even so am I. They are the seede of Abraham, even so am I. They are the ministers of Christ, (I speake as a foole) I am more.[6]

This passage, perhaps, requires some explanation. The first

usage of 'fool' applies to the man who denies God by bringing suffering to Christians. When Paul includes himself as 'fool' he thereby avoids the sin of superiority or spiritual pride in himself. It is interesting that he views the persecutors of Christians as 'ministers of Christ', since of course the early Christian saw even God's alleged enemies as inadvertent instruments of God's purpose. It is also interesting that the passage was read near Shrovetide for in the Liturgy only two references to Fools were made. One was in the Psalm and the other, the Epistle. At the Reformation the Psalm was placed after Epiphany and the Epistle before Shrovetide, and it would seem that the first was an attempt to curb Christmas activity and the second a concession prior to the rigours of Lent.

Innocent folly appears most movingly in those *Mystery Plays* which concern the trial and torturing of Christ; particularly in the Wakefield *Coliphizacio* or *Buffeting* of Christ, and in the York plays of the *Lytsteres* and *Tyllemakers*. In these, Fool-games are the basis of the trial and torture. The Wakefield writer shows a subtle sense of irony. The torturers compare Christ to the seasonal Christmas Fool, who is to be taught a harsher game than customary.

> 2 Tortor   Go we now to our noyte [business] with this fond foyll
> 1 Tortor   We shall teche hym, I wote, a new play of Yoyll [Yule].
>
> [Cawley, p. 87]

However, the Yule game being enacted (the passion and death of Christ) is the fulfilment of the prophecy of his Yule-time birth. On a social level, Christ's birth is the reason for the rejoicing which permitted the pagan Fool games to which the torturers refer. On a deeper level, the torturers—like the persecutors of the Apostles— are the unwitting instruments of God. Therefore, it is they who are *stulti* and Christ is the innocent spirit of Christianity which, though it appears the weakest of forces, overthrows worldly power represented by the torturers. References to Yule would make the irony clear to an audience which indulged in buffeting and other games at that time. And more detail is found in the York plays. In the first (of the *Lytsteres)* Herod presumes Christ to be the local Fool-entertainer or magician and looks foward to seeing water turned into wine and the dead brought to life. When Christ is brought in he is welcomed, and Christ remains silent. The soldiers reassure Herod that the man is taking time to assess the mood of his audience. In other words they take him to be a professional or artificial Fool, who earns his living from entertaining and who, theologically, is the most condemned. Herod, being a trickster himself, is pleased and even when warned that Christ calls himself King of the Jews, Herod interprets this as a King-game[7] in which one of a community is elected king 'in his kith where he comes froo' (line 224). Herod puts away his sceptre— the symbol of his authority— and makes room on the throne for Christ to sit with him. The resulting picture inevitably invokes some Psalm 13 illustrations. In the case of Herod, he enters into the game to the extent that he becomes the Fool which he thinks Christ to be in his attempts to encourage sport. Once all fails, and Christ does not speak throughout, it is taken that Christ is not a witty man, but the dumb or idiot Fool and is taken out for execution. Had Christ said a single word, he would have contributed to the Fool-game that he was placed in and so would have betrayed the Christian aspect of the Fool. The audience would have been fully aware of the two sides to the name and would have been waiting for any possible slip. One can imagine the humour combined with tension when Herod pulls faces and makes gurgling noises to encourage Christ. It would have been essential for the actor playing Christ to keep a straight face. The audience would also have known that the true roles were the reverse of those presented in the play, since the permanence of life after death was the overall theme and by comparison Herod's worldly power is itself a mockery. Whatever the author's general views were regarding secular Fool activity, it is clear that in the *Cycle* they represent devilish influence. Christ's Pauline folly—allowing himself to be taken for an idiot—is emphasised in the second play, where the torturers mock him:

> Hayle! comely kyng, that no kyngdom has kende
> Hayll! vndughty duke, thy dedes are dom [dumb],
> Hayll! man, vnmighty thy men[e] to mende [you need more supporters]

Hayll! lord with-oute lande for to lende,
Hayll! kyng, hayll knave vncommand.
Hayll! freke, without forse thee to fende [defend].   [410-15]

All this is true, yet as the *Cycle* demonstrates, it is a weakness which overturns strength.

Since these plays were in performance by the end of the fourteenth century, it is clear that diametrically opposed views of the Fool were apparent by that time; for whereas the church continued its protection of the witless man, an awareness developed of the need to distinguish such men from their mimics who were beginning to profit from the idiot's immunity from work in the houses of the great. As a discouragement, the church excommunicated all who earned their living in this blasphemous way. The start of explicit association between such men and the devil began with the work of the French theologian, Guilelmus Peraldus in the mid-thirteenth century. M.W. Bloomfield says of Peraldus that he 'is not a mere compiler of quotations but displays a worthy originality . . . the Tractatus had an unquestioned popularity and gave rise . . . to more treatises on the virtues and Sins than it is possible at present to enumerate' (p.124). The Sins of course are caused by weaknesses, called by some *vitiae*[8] and by Peraldus, interestingly, *stultitiae*. The weaknesses lead to Sin and damnation and the correlation which appears is a link between the social *stultus* and the devil. Because of Lucifer's sin of Pride, which caused the initial imperfection in the universe, Pride was held to be the greatest sin. Its rival was Avarice, since Europe became increasingly successful, economically, towards the end of the Middle Ages (Bloomfield, p. 124). Peraldus divided each Sin into an inner and an outer manifestation and, for Pride, he gave two examples of the outer manifestation: the naked and the decorated man. Both were forms of exhibitionism which Peraldus found absurd in view of the mortal nature of the body:

The body of man is as follows:- without food and drink, no power can remain beyond five days, therefore, those who hang useless ornaments from it must be laughable. For just as it would be absurd for men to hang wooden shoes on deformed feet, thus is it absurd for men to decorate themselves. Thirdly, it is seen that men beg decorations . . . to beautify themselves from vile creatures like themselves. A man of good breeding would blush to beg from vile men and would take pains to support the needy who begs from him: so ought a man to blush to beg decorations from vermin and rodents.[9]

He then continues with nudity as the second outward manifestation and he specifically takes the example (quoted in Chapter 1) of the cleric at the Feast of Fools. The man described above, who begs ornaments includes the decorated Fool and Peraldus uses the two types of Fool as examples of the damning Sin of Pride. However, he makes no especial differentiation between artificial Fools and a hypocrite. To his theological way of thinking both are governed by *stultitiae*.

English writers were very much influenced by Peraldus. Chaucer obliquely shows the Fool summoned by the trump of doom in the *Hous of Fame* and in his 'Parson's Tale' the pattern of the sermon follows Peraldus explicitly. The parson says of Pride 'that oon of hem is withinne the herte of man, and that oother is withoute' (line 408). In the rejection of outer decoration, the Parson upbraids those who wear 'sloppes or hainselins'. As Miss Welsford has pointed out, this reference appears to be a pun on the name of the famous French jester of the period, Haincelin Coq, and that it was 'impossible to say whether the fool derived his name from the . . . garment, or whether the vogue was due to the notoriety of the fool' (p. 119). However, the decorated man includes the Fool. Another popular cleric (other than Wyclif)[10] who was influenced by Peraldus was the fifteenth-century writer, John Mirc. In his *Instructions for parish priests* outward display of clothing receives close attention. As well as the lines quoted in Chapter 1, Mirc exhorts priests to resist the same temptation:

> Thow moste forgo for any thynge
> Cuttede clothes and pycked schone . . .
> In honeste clothes thow moste gon,
> Baselard [ornamental dagger] ny bawdryke
>   were thow none.   [42-8]

These writers adopted Peraldus' divisions but the link the French theologian suggested, between Fool and Devil, was

made explicit by William Langland. The type of Fool Langland
was most concerned with was the idiot's mimic, who earned his
living by this impersonation. Eruptions of seasonal activity are
not mentioned. In *Piers Plowman* (*c* 1380) Langland un-
equivocally sees the secular, artificial Fool as the devil's agent.
It also appears, upon examination of the text that Haukyn, the
'Actif' man, is an example used to consider the perplexing
problem of whether the soul of an artificial Fool could be saved.
Three texts exist, known as *A, B* and *C.* In all three Langland
stresses that children and witless men need the protection of
society. In the *A Text* in particular he stresses their innocence
and the impossibility of their damnation, no matter what
mischief they get up to: 'In children and in fools the devil has no
influence over what they do, whether wicked or not'[11] In Passus
10 of the *B Text*, ' folis' are divided into those 'that fauten [lack]
inwitte' and those who feign a lack of wit to gain access to great
houses. The latter are unremittingly attacked. Firstly, Langland argues that they can't even entertain properly. 'Those who
pretend to be fools and live by pretence know no more music or
songs than a miller'.[12] These men are at first called 'fooles
sages', or knowing fools, to distinguish them from the witless
man. However, once the identity of the artifical Fool is established in the text, Langland drops 'sages' and relentlessly
affirms that 'lordes and ladies and legates of holy chirche' who
keep these men are destined for hell, since 'flatterers and fools
are the fiends disciples to entice men through their stories to sin
and harlotry'.[13] Thus, in one work the meaning of 'fool' changes
from the innocent guaranteed eternal salvation to the devil's
disciple equally sure of eternal damnation. Haukyn, Langland's character, freely confesses his lack of musical and narrative gifts; albeit as complaint against the poor reception he
receives, and Langland follows this with a repetition of the
warning against Fools, for thus Haukyn the Active man had
soiled his coat, till Conscience accused him of it in a gentle
manner.[14] Passus 14 studies the attempt by the Virtues to
rescue Haukyn from his allegiance to the devil. At the end of the
Passus, Haukyn appears totally overcome with shame. He
weeps and bewails his state, wishing to have died after baptism,
thereby saving his eternal life. The clamour he makes wakes

Piers and since the section on Haukyn turns out to have only been Piers' dream we never know whether the 'faytour's' repentance was genuine or just another example of his guile, flattery and pretence to superiors. Langland was facing a difficult problem. The artifical Fool was not just a metaphorical abstraction, but a man of flesh and blood and the question of reclaiming his soul was an important one. Since Piers wakes at the crucial moment, it would appear that Langland had no answer except possibly through the intervention of Piers.[15] Langland was the only medieval writer to consider the redemptive problem of the artifical Fool and his popular work may have done much to establish the extreme theological differences in England between the witless man and his mimic.

Moral condemnation of the Fool in France seems not to have had equal power over the Fool's behaviour and the authorities were chiefly concerned with the practical problem of stemming outbursts of activity particularly at the Carnival season[16] when students, who formed fraternities of Fools, but were clearly literate, claimed the idiot's immunity from recrimination for a temporary attack on evils in society, including notable figures, such as the Pope. It appears that in the mid-fifteenth century symbiosis occurred between Carnival purgation and theological or monastic teaching. In the Netherlands town of Deventer a religious school produced three notable thinkers: Thomas à Kempis, Nicholaus of Cusa and (later) Desiderius Erasmus. All three based their writings on a reassertion of Christian folly as the means to salvation. Kempis was the most conventional, relying on the humility such an approach to life demands. However, dramatized satire on the follies of the world found an ally in Nicholaus of Cusa who, in his *Book of the Fool*, used for his spokesman the Fool from society. Ostensibly, the innocent Fool is intended but de Cusa's lack of distinction between the natural and the artificial Fool makes his philosophy ambivalent. The *Ydiota* is given the eloquence to confound philosophers and inevitably one cannot avoid associations with the artifical Fool. De Cusa's purpose was of course the opposite and wished to confound the same over-confidence in knowledge as that rejected by Kempis. It was, perhaps, the confidence de Cusa placed in his own philosophical work,

Coinicidentia Oppositorum, and not theology which led to the secular tone. The philosophy was based on a mathematical hypothesis that the greatest cannot be greater nor less, else it would not be the greatest; and the least cannot be greater or less, else it would not be the least. Therefore, the greatest and least are equal, and, by extension, the Fool can represent God. The *Ydiota* does not remain silent, as Christ does in the York *Mystery* play, but takes the oratorical initiative, confronting the successful philosopher in the market-place with the following declaration:

> I marvel at your pride that wearied with constant reading of innumerable books, you have not yet been led to humility. It is certain that the knowledge of the world is folly before God, and puffs men up, whereas true knowledge humbles them.[17]

It is the philosopher who inadvertantly appears humble when he expresses his ignorance of how to make a Fool reveal his wisdom. The *Ydiota* replies that unlike learned men, who fear to lose their reputations by losing an argument, he knows he is an ignorant idiot and therefore never hesitates to answer any question. Such precocity is very like that of the Carnival Fool, who acts as spokesman in *sermons joyeux* and *sotties*. De Cusa's debate appears to have been both influenced by such figures and afterwards used by *sot* writers in defence of their activities. In the *Dyalogue dung saige & dung fol ignet (Dialogue between a wise man and an ignorant Fool),* written about 1500, the *fol* persuades his would-be wise companion to stay with the Fool society to which they belong and not to return to a comfortable, respectable life on the grounds that it is only the self-acknowledged Fool who is guaranteed salvation.

In England no such arguments prevailed. Moral weight was heavily against the articulate Fool until the Reformation (which was eventually to revive Fool condemnation) gave the English entertainer a brief period of respectability. Before personalities such as Richard Tarlton, William Kemp and Robert Armin, no Fools were sufficiently organized or literate to present their own point of view. The only viewpoint expressed, therefore, was that of the church and moral secular writers. And since the Fool was

always associated with game playing, it is not surprising to find
the fullest examples in Morality plays, once printing was
established. The ignorance of the innocent natural was occasionally used for comic effect; for example, in John Redford's
Wit and Science, where the inability of Ignorance to learn his own
name proves his name. The moral included is the contrast
between this genuine innocence and the wilful folly of a fallen
man of wit. Most writers were concerned with displaying the
evil side of the artificial Fool and what is most surprising is that
John Heywood, who sympathised more with French comic
theatre, concurred with the established view when writing
directly about Fools in his play of *Wytty and Wytless.* To begin
with, the spokesman for the baptismally innocent, witless man
says:

> . . . from owre forfathers syn orygynall,
> Baptysm sealyth us all a quyttans generall;
> Wherby tyll wytt take root of dyscernynge,
> And betweene good and yll geve perfyght warnyng,
> Wherever innosents, innosency dyspewt,
> For thowghtes wordds or dedes God doth none yll ympewt.
> Where God gyvyth no dyscernyng God taketh none acownte.
>   [de la Bère, p. 129]

This assertion corresponds with the medieval view of natural
Fools, and the *wytless* man avoids de Cusa's trap of claiming to
be more humble relying instead on the doctrine that he has the
passport to heaven. However, unlike the writer of the French
Dyalogue, Heywood does not leave the argument here, and it is
indicative of the Reformist faith in knowledge that St Jerome is
represented at the end to counter these claims with the
assurance that the pleasures, both in this life and the next, are
greater for the man capable of learning.

Another aspect of the evil associated with the artificial Fool
leads to the origin of the name 'Vice' for the leading character,
who is frequently malevolent, in later sixteenth-century
Morality plays. Theological condemnation supports F. H.
Mares' conclusion that the Vice was 'already established as a
stage clown before he appears in the morality' (Mares p. 11).
Perhaps it would be more accurate to say that he was already a

well-known social entertainer. Just as the early evidence shows the Fool as leader of the games and dances[18] the Vice is made leader of the scripted action, until his demise. The dress of the later Vices was varied but I agree with Mares, also, on the point that until about 1550 the Vice wore Fool's dress. In the list of named Vices Mares gives, only four appear before 1555 and nineteen between 1555 and 1579; and all of the first four are Fools. One is Flatterie in David Lyndsay's *Satyre of the thrie estaitis,* who introduces himself as follows:

> Make room sirs, so that I may run
> See, see where I'm back again
> Decked out in many colours . . .
> What do you say, sirs; arn't I gay?
> Don't you see Flatterie, your own fool
> Who's come to join this new festivity
> Wasn't I here with you at Yule?[19]

The reference to his absence since Christmas was a joke on the seasonal licence allowed to the Fool for the text he appears in here was performed in summer out of doors and he jokes about his sufferings since Christmas: 'Tossed on the sea ever since Yule's day' (line 609). The moral of the *Satyre* is one which strives to destroy the serious mischief of the Fool, but, in accordance with seasonal practice, Flatterie escapes.

Two other named Vices are from John Heywood's farces, *The play of Love,* in which the Vice claims to be a Fool (line 721) and *The play of the Weather,* where it is generally thought that Mery Report—wearing 'lyght . . . araye' —is played as a Fool. Lastly, it might appear that Bale's *The three Laws* proves an exception, since 'six vices' are specified in the *dramatis personae:* five have male clerical dress and the sixth, interestingly, is a man dressed as a witch. However, there is a seventh character, the Vices' leader, called Infidelity. It is Infidelity who takes the initiative in obstructing Reform. His language is full of the coarse wit of a Fool, he is called Fool in the text and is eventually sent to Hell by *Deus Pater.* In the action of the play we find again six men led by a Fool and confirmation that Lydgate's dance motif became a symbol of fall from reason is found in other Morality plays.[20] The mid-sixteenth century then became an interesting period of transition. Accounts of Vices dressed as Fools change to those of Fools dressed as Vices. In the Revels' Account for 1555 the entry reads: 'One frock yolowe velet all cheveroned with brode gardes . . . with one hed pece . . . for a vyees [sic] to a play after to the lorde mysruell' (Mares, p. 15). The frock was typical Fool's dress[21] but the mention of chevrons introduces a separate feature. The separation is even clearer in the 1552 Revels' Accounts where two records tell us that the court Fool, John Smith, wore a Vice's coat to which was added a 'dissardes' or Fool's hood.[22] And so it appears that distinctions were gradually drawn between Vice and Fool costume during the 1550s. Peter Happé remarks that it was after 1560 that the Vice 'in its most developed form' came into existence (p. 161), and it may be more than coincidental that after this date alternative dress appears, which varied from play to play. The wooden dagger, carried by the 1300 naked Fool, was kept by the Vices as a comic property and was so effective that Harlequin in the eighteenth century retained it for his own comic, theatrical battles.

It may also be more than coincidence that at the time when the Vice became a separate character from the Fool, the Fool himself began to enjoy growing popularity among respectable thinkers of the day; and in plays the Fool *per se* developed those attributes of social, seasonal festivity exploited by Lyndsay's Flatterie. For example, in the anonymous play, *Misogonus (c* 1564-6), the Fool, Cacurgus—from the same root as *cachinor*— plays on the theological distinction between the innocent and the artificial by gaining entrance to Philogonus' house on pretence of being the former and he is given free reign by the author to rule the household. The play was written for the Christmas season and so use is made of the liberty given the Fool by society at that time to entertain freely in the scripted play. Finally, when Cacurgus is expelled, the audience is brought swiftly back to these social realities. A Fool turned out of doors in mid-winter had little chance of survival. Cacurgus laments: 'and I might be but wintered this yeare I woud neare care/A god helpe to William now thart put to thy nede' (IV, iii, 13-14). By contrast, Flatterie saw his expulsion in summer as a triumph not defeat. In both cases the authors use seasonal practice as the basis for the Fool's reaction, and while scripted plays kept to the old seasonal times for playing, the social Fool's traditional freedoms were an intrinsic part of those plays: copying, as it were, unscripted Fool-drama. The moral rationale was as follows. The play was part of the winter or summer periods of Misrule, during which the artificial Fool had the leading role, and yet with the background of moral purpose the texts work towards the elimination of their Fools against which the Fools, not unnaturally, oppose themselves. The whole of the second half of *Misogonus* is a battle between order, instigated by an innocent country rustic or 'cloun' and Cacurgus' disorder. Hence, until festivity became a dominant theme in comic drama at the end of the sixteenth century (as Barber shows in relation to Shakespeare) the theme of festivity runs counter to that of morality.

The gradual change in respectable attitudes eliminated the concepts of innocent and wicked and replaced them with the single idea that a Fool was a natural if he was a recognized Fool. The change began with Sir Thomas More. His *Utopia* is perhaps the earliest English work which upholds toleration for all Fools: witless and aritificial alike. He relates a tale of a parasite who attempted to win favour by mimicking the witless man. Without approval or disapproval, More simply observes that the man's inability to imitate was more cause for amusement than his imitation. 'There was one great parasite who wished to be seen imitating a fool, but he mimicked in such a way, and his jests were so feeble that it could truly be said that he himself was more laughed at than his sayings.'[23] More was an exception—writing in the first half of the century. Erasmus' *Praise of Folly* was published in Paris in 1511 and translated into English in 1549, but it appears clear that the translator's purpose was not to present the mosaic of folly of the original, but to show the poor the disadvantages of being in power, and so to induce contentment with their lot (Swain, p. 141). It is particularly notable that in the English version certain emphases are changed. The most important is the editing out of Erasmus' conflation of idiot Fools and artificial Fools and the replacement with traditional church approval of the witless man only. Erasmus put in a heading, '*Moriones & fatui omnium felicissimi*', which means 'witty fools and natural fools are the happiest of men', and Chaloner, the translator, changed the heading to read, 'Naturall fooles the happiest of all men'.

Change in attitude was more fully effected by the example of two Fool-personalities: Richard Tarlton and Robert Armin. Baskervill says of the jig-maker, Tarlton, that he was the first Fool-actor 'to achieve a fame that lived and exert an influence that was recognized for generations' (p. 96). The most striking example of this influence was the effect Tarlton had on the opinion of the churchman, Thomas Bastard. Although the Reverend was thoroughly familiar with the standard attitude of his profession towards Tarlton's profession, he was, nevertheless sufficiently impressed to invert the concept of folly into an art capable of excellence. Bastard wrote (in Tarlton's voice):

> Who taught me pleasant follies, can you tell?
> I was not taught and yet I did excell.
> T''is hard to learne without a president,
> T''is harder still to make folly excellent.
> I sawe, yet had no light to guide mine eyes
> I was extold for that which all despise.[24]

Twenty-nine years after Tarlton's death his influence was still remembered in the following epitaph:

> . . . all clownes since have been his apes
> Earst he of clownes to learne still sought,
> But now they learne of him they taught;
> By art far past the principall,
> That counterfet is so worth all.[25]

Since 'clownes' is used in its original rustic sense of clumsy, innocent or ignorant Fool, the anonymous writer not only abandons theological distinctions, but inverts their causal relationship. As one writer (thought to have been Robert Armin) wrote two years after Tarlton's death, Tarlton defied categories. 'Well, howsoever either naturall, or artificiall, or both, he was a mad merry companion . . . loved by all.'[26] And finally, it was the writings of Robert Armin and perhaps his influence on Shakespeare which completely rid the Fool of any ominous associations and, temporarily at least, established him as a legitimate part of society. Like the French *sots*, Armin was literate enough to become a commentator on society and the first biographer of other Fools. In line with the tradition of six led by a seventh, Armin wrote *Foole vpon Foole or Six Sortes of Sottes* and in the conclusion says the worst that can happen to him is to be included with his subjects. The biographies of less known Fools are short but the approach consolidates the 'natural' as justified member of a household or town. Clearly there is a difference between the witlessness of John of the Hospital (subtitled 'A Verry Foole') and the intelligence of Will Somer ('A Merry Foole'), yet in the Preface all six are called 'fooles naturall' and one story which concerns a violent Fool, Jack Oates, shows how far toleration could go. To tease Oates, a minstrel was dressed as a rival. When Oates saw the usurper the injuries he gave him were such as couldn't be repaired, but the only moral Armin draws is the interesting one that 'Fooles artificial' such as the minstrel, must accept their penance 'sign'd him by Iack Oates'. Theological knowledge is in the background but scaled down to worldly terms in which the retribution waiting for the artificial is exacted by the man with the right to the title.

One further point Armin raises is that the artificial Fool, particularly one who was employed in the theatre, had as much right and more to social dignity as any other man. C.S. Felver suggests that *Qvips vpon Qvestion* came to be written because Armin was 'stung . . . by the implication that his actions in real life were as foolish as his actions in the theatre' (p.29). Therefore, in 'He who plays the foole', Armin wrote:

> True it is, he playes the Foole indeed;
> But in the play he plays it as he must:
> Yet when the Play is ended, then his speed
> Is better then the pleasure of thy trust:
>> For he shall have what thou that time has spent,
>> Playing the foole, thy folly to content.[27]

Not only is the Fool vindicated, but the term 'fool' turned on his detractors, who pay to see their own follies enacted and performers like Armin play 'the Wise man then, and not the Foole,/That wisely for his lyuing so can do' (fol. C.2.v.). By the end of the sixteenth century, therefore, we see a complete reversal from the medieval concept of the artificial Fool. Further, the implications that all men but the Fool were fools for paying was to be extended in the seventeenth century into the statement that all men but dramatic poets (who were forbidden to practise their craft after 1642) were mad. The earlier concepts of evil in pretended stupidity and the innocence of the idiot, which are essential to an understanding of the Fool's place in medieval society, never returned.

The polarization between Fool as wise man and Fool as evil is a paradox which has been much enjoyed and appears at first sight to have no resolution. The reason appears to be that Erasmus' brilliant *Praise of folly* has understandably been the most attractive point of departure for Fool studies and he has inspired illuminating examinations of continental literature and some of Shakespeare's work. Enid Welsford's perception that *King Lear* was structured according to saturnalian principles follows her study of *sotties* and *The praise of folly*. It also appears, though it is not said in precise words, that the protean nature of folly which informs Barbara Swain's work was, in part, due to the stimulus of Erasmus. However, Erasmus was not a representative theologian. The satire in his *Praise of folly* was considered near blasphemous in England, even by Elizabethan satirists. Erasmus himself enjoyed paradox and he deliberately dispensed with distinctions between innocent and artificial Fools. Because of his background he had no need to make clear his paradoxes, though, today, Fool studies which do not do this inevitably produce inconsistencies. On page 4 Barbara Swain asserts that folly is 'a condition of witlessness or ignorance or both'. However, she also notes that the French play, *Les Sobres Sots,* separates the 'wise' and 'foolish' of moral terminology from that of the 'innocent'. These distinctions, (which Erasmus deliberately ignored) were more than an accidental dramatic device, but were fundamental to church attitudes in both France and England and pervaded social attitudes in England. And since, in England, clerical writings were almost the only articulated opinions, orthodox theology is essential to an understanding of the two kinds of Fool and their position in medieval society.

CHAPTER 3

The rise of the Fool

No new proof is needed to establish the popularity of Fools in the sixteenth century. The works of Enid Welsford, C.R. Baskervill, Walter Kaiser and William Willeford attest to this fact. The information is everywhere; in records, accounts, stories of seasonal entertainments and plays. And since it was the growth of printing as well as greater social stability which led to the sudden profusion of information, we can see that it is more likely that unrecorded Fool customs existed before 1500 than that these customs were suddenly imported from the continent. Fools of the sixteenth century have, in the twentieth century, received courtly, professional and psychological attention. This chapter will concentrate on the rural origins from which most of the famous personalities derived for the ending of the Wars of the Roses allowed eccentric characters, who might have lain in rural oblivion, to become the focus of entertainment. The editor of John Heron's Account books for the court of Henry VII, Sidney Anglo, points out that 'the most frequently mentioned entertainers . . . are the fools. Fools abound from 1 January 1492, when 'my Lorde Privy Seall fole' was rewarded with 10s., to 4 December 1508 when John 'late the King of Castelles fole' received 40s.'[1] Throughout these accounts (1492-1508) a number of Fools from Europe are mentioned and illustrate the celebration of a general if temporary peace. However, the most well-known Fools were native and their rural origins are mentioned in passing in most of their brief biographies. There are also indications that talent-spotting for Fools was part of a nobleman's employment while travelling through the countryside. For example, a letter concerning serious matters from Thomas Bedyll to Thomas Cromwell, written 26 January 1535/6, concludes as follows:

ye knowe the Kinges grace hath one old fole: Sexton as good as might be whiche bicause of aige is not like to cõtinew. I have spied one yong fole at Croland whiche in myne opinion shalbe muche mor pleasaunt than ever Sexten was . . . and he is not past XV yere old/Whiche is every day newe to the herere . . . albeit I mi self have but smal delectation in folys. [PRO SP 1.101, p.192.]

The last comment reads as respectful acknowledgement of the correct attitude in view of the churchman to whom Bedyll was writing and the identity of Bedyll's Fool is never subsequently revealed. It is possible that Bedyll's good intentions did not come to fruition. Some household Fools were of higher birth. A man proven *purus idiota* (a simple idiot) by a jury became the property of the Crown, and his person and property could be bestowed on someone else. Applications were known as 'begging for a fool' and with the inducement of property, it seems that the law, *de idiota inquirendo* (examining into the witlessness of a man) was open to abuse. In the time of James I, Lord North 'begged' a member of the wealthy Bladwell family though there were doubts as to whether 'old Bladwell' was in fact insane. Bladwell conveyed an appropriate metaphoric protest at his situation when he and his master were visiting a neighbour. Left alone in a room hung with tapestry, Bladwell looked closely at the pictures in it, 'spied a foole at last in the hanging, and, without delay, draws his knife, flies at the foole, cuts him clean out and lays him on the floor'. When asked why he had done such an uncivil thing, Bladwell replied that he had, rather, done the man a favour for, had Lord North seen the Fool he would have begged him and the owner would have lost the whole tapestry.[2] This suggests a frustrated sanity and Bladwell may not have been alone.

However, the happier stories of the famous court Fools were, more often than not, about personalities brought to court from the country. It was the Somersetshire man, Will Somers, who could joke Henry VIII out of most of his difficult moods. In his lifetime, Somers was loved by the people for intervening on behalf of the poor. One day Somers fell asleep against a post and an old woman, fearing he might fall and injure himself, not only placed a cushion behind him, but actually tied him to the post. One other story Armin tells is of Somer's uncle appearing at

Greenwich with a petition against enclosure of common land in Shropshire. Realising the rough dress wouldn't please Henry, Somers dressed the old man in his own 'best fooles coate . . . cappe and all'. Henry saw that Will had found himself another Fool and became merry looking forward to the 'sport', which began with Somers saying 'Harry heare me tell thee a tale, and I will make thee rich, and my uncle shall be made rich by thee'. After listening, Henry asked where his own self interest lay, to which Will replied 'The poore will pray for thee . . . and thou shalt bee rich in heaven, for on earth thou art rich already'. As Enid Welsford says, one of the King's and the Fool's favourite games was improvising rhymes and capping one another's verses. One day the King, Cardinal Wolsey and Will were riding along together and passed a place where Henry had a mistress. The King asked Somers if he could cap these verses:

> Within yon tower
> There is a flower
> That hath my heart.

Apparently Somers gave such a bawdy response that the chronicler refused to set it down. Henry was amused, but Wolsey attempted to rebuke the Fool, saying:

> A rod in the School
> And a whip for the fool
> Are always in season.
>
> A halter and rope
> For him that would be Pope
> Against all right and reason,
> [Welsford, *The Fool*, p. 256]

was the Fool's immediate reply. 'At which the Cardinal bit his lip.' Armin tells of how Will tricked Wolsey into repaying his debts to the poor by giving them ten pounds of the Cardinal's money. 'The King laught at the jest, and so did the Cardinal for a shew, but it grieved him to jest away ten pounds'. The fame of Somers lasted after his death. Thomas Nashe wrote an entertainment called 'Summers last Will and Testament' with deliberate pun on the name, and Samuel Rowley wrote a play which incorporated the greatest myth about the Fool. That was that it had been Somers who had discovered Wolsey's treachery to the king. Somers and Patch (the natural who had once belonged to Wolsey until the Cardinal had tired of him) stole down to the King's cellars to help themselves to wine. When a hogshead failed to produce any, Will was said to have broken it open and found it full of melted-down gold, stolen from the King by the churchman. Somers' reputation earned him a place in plays and Enid Welsford points out that his talents were of the standard of a professional Fool, but the period in which Somers lived was too early for him to have had the freedom to entertain in public. Fools were still owned by their masters, and despite Somers' intelligence and the respect Henry showed for him, Somers' life was bounded by the court: amusing the King and eating and sleeping with the spaniels.

Later in the century Somers' fellow-countryman, Richard Tarlton, was also brought to London and as well as his position as court Fool, he had the influential professional life in society. Initially, though, he too was brought from Shropshire to Queen Elizabeth. Robert Fuller's well-known account reads that Tarlton 'was in the field keeping his father's swine, when a servant of Robert, Earl of Leicester, passing this way . . . was so pleased with his *happy unhappy* answers, that he brought him to court, where he became the most famous jester to Queen Elizabeth' (Welsford, p. 282). Little is known of Tarlton's biography. The *Jestbook* attributed to him lacks wit and one can only trust Fuller's further assurance that 'much of [Tarlton's] merriment lay in his very looks . . . words, spoken by another, would hardly move a merry man to smile [but] uttered by him, would force a sad soul to laughter' (Welsford, p. 283). Also, Baskervill makes it clear that much of Tarlton's talent lay in his feet. As a jig-dancer, Tarlton did much to make the Fool's dance separate from that of the Morris dancers, and this will be picked up later on. By contrast, the Scots Fool who went to court from the country, Jemmy Camber, moved smiles through his lack of physical agility. Like the Fool of Bedyll's letter, Camber was only a boy when he was taken to Edinburgh:

> This fat foole was a Scot borne, brought vp

In *Sterlin,* twenty miles from Edinburgh:
Who being but young was for the King caught vp
Seru'd this Kings father all his life time through.[3]

In all these stories there is some support for Enid Welsford's fear that coercion rather than persuasion was used to transport the Fools from their rural homes. On the other hand, Alexander Barclay in about 1510 showed in his *Eclogues* that the increased prospects for the countryman at court could have been an attraction. In the poem the young shepherd, Corydon, expresses his intention of leaving the hard life tending sheep to become a lord's entertainer, and so live comfortably. Barclay dismisses such an ambition according to the moral trends of his time: 'That foole were worth a bable and a hood/Which would choose the worst, perceiving wel the good'.[4] Even without the moral implications, Sidney Anglo also felt that 'pleying the fole' could cause a dangerous change in the performer's status. Heron's accounts of Henry VII's payments record that on 4 October 1504 Watt the Luter was paid 13/8d for playing the fool and a month later received only 10s for *being* the Fool. What is even more puzzling is that the money was given 'to Richard Nevill for Watt the fole'. This indicates that the Fool concerned was considered an idiot, like Dick, whose master received his payments for looking after the Fool. It is possible that Richard Neville was one of the music masters for a lutanist must have had some intelligence.

The other area for Fools in society is the continuing one of rural traditions. These continually appear in the sixteenth century in connection with the Morris dance which, I believe, was in existence either under a different name or no name[5] from the Middle Ages. Decisive evidence appears in two separate accounts which were made of Henry VII's Christmas entertainment of 1494. The *Great Chronicle of London* includes the description of a startling, lively dance by Spanish courtiers, which was performed with such energy that their 'spangyls of goold & othyr of their garnisshys ffyl ffrom them Right habundantly' (Thornley, p. 252). On the surface this appears to support the belief that it was about this period that the Morris was imported into England from Spain. However, Heron's accounts mention that four days before, men had been paid 40s.

for 'pleying of the mourice dance' and so the two events must have been separate, and though the men's dance may have been influenced by foreign demonstrations, the custom was already indigenous. The reason for the sudden proliferation of records was the renewed peace and increasing literacy. Records of financial transactions appear in many major towns as well as at court, and rural folk games were adopted by the church as a means of collecting money for stipends and church repairs. E. Hobhouse's details of customs in and around Bath show that the King game gave way to games held under the auspices of an elected Robin Hood, who performed the same role as the 'King'.[6] The first detailed accounts come from Kingston-upon-Thames. The Churchwardens' Account book for 1509/10 lists a profusion of costumes and expenses for characters. The entries cover several folios and it is not clear whether it was the year of Henry VIII's accession (which was a difficult one for Henry) or the following year which saw this surge of celebrations. Among many expenses appear the following:

paid for mete & drynke for ye mores daunsers	ijd
payd sylv ⁻ paper for mores dauncers	vijd
paid for mete and drynke for ye mores daunsers on corpus xti day	iiijd
payd for ye foles Cote	xiiijd
payd for vj peyre of shone for ye mores dauncers	iiijs
paid to a tabore	vd
paid for kendall for Robyn hodes cote	xvd
paid for the frere cote	iijs
paid for litell john ⁻ is cote	viijs iiijd
paid for the bote hire goyng uppe to Walton Kyngham	xd
paid for the visitacion ⁻ at lethered	viijd
paid to mayde marion for hir labor for ij yere	ijs[7]

Maid Marion was here played by a woman and received more than twice as much as the musician for her two years' playing. Women who didn't mind the rough and strenuous games and dances were not precluded from taking part. The 'Queen' at Kingston, when they had one, was often played by a woman, and in 1599, when William Kemp made his famous journey from London to Norwich, the only follower to keep up with him over a mile was a woman. Since the early Kingston accounts cover two years' expenses for Maid Marion, it would seem that 1509 and 1510 are combined in the lists of games. The mixture of games at Kingston is what one would expect. The Robin Hood team with Little John and Friar Tuck are placed alongside the Morris and both needed a Maid Marion. Robert Laneham said in 1575 that the 'olde style' Morris required 'six daunsearz Maid Marion and the foole' (Furnivall, ed. p. 23). Comparison with the accounts gathered by Hobhouse suggests that the Kingston games were held under the auspices of an elected Robin Hood but the entertainments were not limited to a Robin Hood play. Also, the Kingston team travelled (as did nineteenth-century teams) either to compete or to collect money at Walton and Leatherhead, despite the fact that Walton has its own king-led games.

It could have been more than coincidence that almost immediately after the revelling in and around Kingston, the Morris rose to brief heights as a court Mask at Henry's Richmond home, close to Kingston, for the Christmas of 1510/11. The Mask there at Epiphany was a Morris, not brought in from outside but performed by Henry's own 'hynsmen'. We have two descriptions: one is of the audience impression of splendour, written by a guest, Edward Halle. The other is a breakdown of fabric and costs, kept by Henry's accountant, Richard Gibson. Firstly, Halle wrote:

> Agaynste the xii daye or the daye of the Epiphanie at nighte, before the banket in the Hall at Richmond, was a pageaut deuised like a mountayne, glisteringe by night, as though it had been all of golde and set with stones, on the top of the whiche mountayne was a tree of golde, the braunches and bowes frysed with gold, spredynge on euery side ouer the mountayne, with Roses and Pomegarnettes, the which mountayne was with Vices brought vp towardes the kyng, & out of thesame came a ladye, appareiled in cloth of golde, and the children of honor called the Henchmen, which were freshly disguised, and daunced a Morice befoe the kyng. And that done, reentred the moutaine and then it was drawen backe, and then was the wassail or banket brought in, and so brake vp Christmas.[8]

Not surprisingly, Gibson wrote more prosaically. A 'Moriske' was

> dancyd be þe kynges yong gentyllmen as hynsmen and thereto a lady for

þe weche was pre paryd and bowght . . . erthen vesselles/hoges brystylles/
Pynke/venegyr/kotyn kandelles/. . .bokelles/garteres/dartes/kotun clothes
/a ladyll turnd [the Fool's wooden collecting spoon]/chest bordes . . ./
metyll belles of sundrie sortes/whyt sarsenete/crymsyn sarsenet[9]

and many thousands of spangles which, with the bells, decorated the dancers' clothes. The Fool's coat was an elaborate
work of red and white sarsenet, lined with buckram. The four
hanging points of his coat were each hung with twelve bells,
nine dozen bells hung from the Fool's arms and legs and, since
the dancers were all similarly encumbered, one imagines that
this dance was more stately than any Kingston model. Also,
fourteen buckles set with bells are entered in the accounts.
Assuming to each man a pair of legs, the whole dance com-
prised seven men, one of whom was the Fool. The team of Fool
plus six dancers found itself transported from its rustic origins
in the Middle Ages to the centre of courtly attention.

After this one display the dance returned to a less sophisticated audience. Another version can be pieced together from
the accounts for Henry's 1514/15 *Mask of Venus and Beauty*, but
on the whole the dance with Fool is recorded in city accounts—
such as those of Reading and the City of London—, in plays,
and in personal memoirs. In courtly entertainments the Fool's
role was for a while that of attendant to the elected Christmas
Lord of Misrule. The two greatest Revels were those just before
Edward VI's untimely death in 1553. The dignified lawyer,
George Ferrers, was the Lord for 1551/2 and 1552/3, and Fools
were placed in attendance upon him. The ageing Will Somers
was one and in 1552, John Smith (who wore the Vice's coat and
dissardes hood) took part with two other Fools in mock combat
with Ferrers.[10] The diary of Henry Machyn contains a description of the whole of Ferrer's mock court processing through the
City of London on 4 January. In 1551/2 one Morris, which
appears to have been the contribution of the City of London, is
mentioned. However, there was greater splendour the following
year, when the Lord's procession was met by the Sheriff of
London's, and the Sheriff went before Ferrers bearing a sword
of honour. The Sheriff's retinue was more modest than that of
Ferrers, who displayed a large part of the court behind him.

After the courtiers came various groups, 'doctors proclaiming my Lorde great', and all dressed in the same livery. Finally came 'trumpeters, taburs, drumes, and flutes and fulles and ys mores dansse' (Machyn, p. 28). So the court Fool attendants were in separate category from the Fools of the dance. And the practice of 'Royal Jesters' processing on May day takes place at Knutsford today. In the sixteenth century the Fool was gradually winning respectability and individuality in plays and through solo performances which showed great skill in innovation, such as those of Richard Tarlton. Supporting this development was the practice of electing Christmas Lords in both the universities and in the Inns of Court, which continued after Edward VI's death, since of course the Elizabethan playwrights were initially those men who had been educated at one of these establishments. F.S. Boas remarks with surprise that the early statutes of St John's College, Cambridge make no mention of a Christmas *dominus* (Lord), but as late as 1545, Henry VIII's orders include 'a remarkable passage . . . ordaining that each Fellow in his turn shall be elected "dominus", and shall on no account refuse to carry out the duties of the office' (Boas, p.8). The honour of being *dominus* carried the difficult responsibility of keeping order during an irresponsible season and was not an office for fooling. However, Fools' costumes recur in the Inventories of the period. The 1548 Indenture includes 'an old torne fooles cootes of div'se colors [and] a fooles coote w_th checker Work of grene Red & White'. Another document, which is probably an earlier one lists 'iij folys cotys, ij pykkytt [peaked] hattys [and] v folys hodys' (Billington, pp. 6-8). At Oxford there was never any enforcement of a Christmas Lord. The decree brought in by Queen Mary Tudor and her Spanish husband, Philip, in 1553/4 at Christ Church states limitations on the students' activities. The Lord was to be allowed xiij_s iiij_d yearly 'and nomore', and limitations were placed on the new (i.e. classic) dramas which were the mainspring of the Elizabethan drama. Evidence for the prominent part of the Fool surfaces in an attack by Ponet, Bishop of Winchester, on the Roman Catholic controversialist, Thomas Martyn. In 1556 Ponet wrote 'in playing the Christmas lords minion in Oxford in thy foles coat . . . thou didest learne thy boldness, and lost thy witt, and began to put off all shame and to put on all impudencye' (Boas, p. 7). When, in 1607, the Fool at St John's College, Oxford, accidentally broke the Prince's staff before a play proper began, the writer used the incident as an apologia—superstitiously tongue-in-cheek—should the ensuing piece not please.[11] In the Cambridge City records there is one example which links the Fool with the office of Lord and shows Fools taking to the fairgrounds for survival. In 1638 an accusation was brought against one Richard Williams, musician, who made himself Lord Tapps after the decease of John Lyon and

> sayeth he hath nothing vnder seale to show for that office. he had his L[or]d Tapps coate & a fether in hatt & had much a doe to keepe his hat of. He was accused of causing public disorder this fayer by taking vppon him in this dangerous tyme to be Lord tapps & cryde about the fayer contrary to that complaint was made against him . . . & attyred his self in his fooles coate & w[i]th his . . . staff & bell . . . hath drawne to gether greate flock'[es] & multitud[es] of people to follow him in crowd[es] after his musick.[12]

The dangerous time referred to the increasing civil disturbances as Charles I and Parliament grew more openly antagonistic. It was not surprising that any public spokesman was vetted by the authorities. This latter-day Pied Piper indicates the reluctance for Fools to give way to opposition. Attacks had begun on their professional activities as soon as they were established. The most famous and colourful denunciation came from Phillip Stubbes in 1583 (Furnivall, ed.). However, their box-office attraction outweighed censure. Marston and Rowley played to the groundlings' taste for dancing and Fools and Dekker included a similar character, called Firke, in *The Shoemakers' holiday*, which played before the Queen in 1599. *Jacke Drums entertainment* (Marston, 1600) contains a Fool as witty spokesman for the Morris dances, and by his repartee he elicits money from the bystanders. The difficulty of weaning audiences from their predilection was frequently cause for complaint from Ben Jonson (*The staple of news* 1625) and John Fletcher (*The faithful Shepherdess* 1608). The City authorities intervened in 1548, when the Midsummer Watch with its nightly procession and feasting in the City of London was discontinued and, in 1552, 'a goodly May-polle' (Machyn, p.20) was taken down and broken on the order of the Lord Mayor. In an abortive attempt to divert seasonal enthusiasm, civic processions were encouraged in place of traditional entertainments. The organisation required for the Misdummer Watch was channelled into the Lord Mayor's shows. However, many regretted the passing of the Midsummer revels. The positive, saturnalian principle of festivity, which C.L. Barber explores in relation to Shakespeare's early comedies sometimes worked in practice. As Stow relates: 'neighbours that, before being at controuersie, were there, by the labour of others, reconciled'.[13] From records of the Watch we find confirmation that the Morris, with its Fool, was never confused with Morisco pageants. The dance game was always performed by independent, semi-professional, seasonal players. The clearest example comes from the Drapers' Accounts for 1521. Their principal pageant was 'A King of More[s] & L moryans'. There are detailed records of the extensive costs arising from this battle display, which included the storming of the Moors' castle. After appears the modest addition, 'It. to Robert Graves for a morysdánce & ij mynstrelle[s] riding at there own coste . . . paid for the more[s] daúnce for bothe nyghte[s] . . . '[14]

It was only between about 1580 and 1620 that the Fool gained some official respectability. Those Fools who enhanced the reputation of the profession, Tarlton, Kemp and Armin, moved in all circles: popular society, professional theatre and the court. For the most part their skills were the clowning arts of dancing, tumbling and singing, all of which were adopted by those Fools who survived in the fairgrounds in the following centuries. Baskervill notes that 'a number of symbolic names seem to have developed' for the Fool. The names mentioned are all to do with food. Baskervill includes Cob in *Everyman in his humour*; Pickleherring in the Revesby folk-play text of 1789 and 1799[15], and 'typical sixteenth century figures are Jack-a-Lent and Jack Pudding' (pp. 93-4). Jack-a-Lent is described by Machyn in 1553, but we have no explicit information that Jack Pudding was current usage in aural tradition until the end of the sixteenth century. As far as contemporary writers were concerned, clown and Fool seem to have been specific descriptions in themselves. The clown was understood to be the country bumpkin or 'cloun' and many well-known clowns kept their country clothes and manners. In the *Newes out of Puratorie* Richard Tarlton is recognized 'by his sute of russet, his buttond cap, his tabor'[16] and not by a Fool's parti-coloured coat. Similarly, the illustration of William Kemp in *Kemps Nine Daies Wonder* shows him wearing large streamers from his shoulders but, otherwise, doublet and hose of the period. The performance of both men was based on the behaviour of the clown and it was in these early days of Fool freedom that Sir Philip Sidney complained of the clown thrust by head and shoulders into tragedies. C.S. Felver gives the most comprehensive summary of their style and talents.

> The greatest Elizabethan reputation for clowning was held by Richard Tarlton (d. 1588), playwright, ballad-maker, fencer, tumbler, dancer, impromptu rhymer, and witty improviser. Tarlton's usual line was that of the rustic fellow . . . and he often carried a great bag, a large bat, or a pipe and tabor. His naturally ludicrous appearance, flat-nosed and squint-eyed, was enhanced by tricks like standing on the toe or repeating popular bits of "business".
>
> Second only to Tarlton . . . was William Kemp (d. 1603), who had all of Tarlton's attributes excepting those of fencer and impromptu rhymer and was especially renowned as a jig-maker and dancer. He was, perhaps more than Tarlton, the country rustic who made people laugh at his ignorance, his violation of the language, and his Dogberry-like dullness.   [p. 9]

Neither man was genuinely witless and both used apparent stupidity as the trademark of their artifical fooling. Both men were literate. Kemp is credited with having written *A knack to know a Knave,* which contains Dogberry-like abuse of the language such as 'now let us constult among ourselves/How to misbehave ourselves to the King's worship'. Felver suggests that Shakespeare improved on this style in Dogberry in *Much ado about nothing,* with Kemp playing the part. It seems that though his personality was suitable for characters such as this and Costard in *Love's labours lost,* his inability to say no more than the text set down, led to his dismissal from the company of Chamberlain's Men in 1599. In 1598 Kemp was attacked by name in the play, *Pilgrimage* to *Parnassus* (pt. 1, v 662-9) and the date is conveniently close to the probable date of Kemp's departure from the professional theatre. The jig or Morris dance which he undertook from London to Norwich in 1599 may well have been a way of restoring his personal reputation and popularity. Today, it is the graphic account of his journey, which Kemp had printed in 1600, that we remember him by.

Not very much is known of Tarlton, other than his physiognomy and his talents. Tradition has it that he made Robert Armin his heir 'to enjoy my clownes sute after me' (Felver, p. 11) and he is known to have belonged to the Queen's company of players. The plays he appeared in were not the famous ones and his fame lies in the inventiveness of his jigs and since he was skilled at extemporizing on local gossip, it appears he frequently rescued the company by his solo performances. ' "While the quenes players lay in Worcester city to get money, it was his custome to sing extempore of theames given to him" ', and the audience frequently came just to see his performance *'at the end of the play'* (Baskervill, p.99). This coda to the main play which he made famous was either song or dance or a combination of both. None of Tarlton's extempore jigs appear to have survived[17] and Kemp has the advantage of a number of his pieces recorded in the Stationer's Register. By 1599 there were:

> the thirde and last part of *Kempes* Jigge
> A Plesant newe Jigge of the Broome-man
>   [called in the margin] Kempes
> master Kemps Newe Jigge of the kitchen stuffe woman
> Kempe newe Jygge betwixt, a souldier and a Miser
>   and Sym the clown "Singing Simpkin"
>   [Baskervill, p. 108]

Kemp's greatest feat, that of dancing from London to Norwich in nine days of dancing—there were rests *en route*—was attacked by rivals as a fraud. Kemp declared it was such accusations which caused him to set down the details in his *Nine Daies Wonder*. At the opening Kemp calls himself one 'that hath spent his life in mad jigs and jests', yet at the end he rounds upon the 'ballad-jig-makers' who had slandered him. This contradiction is indicative of the change which the jig underwent. The jigs listed as Kemp's all have traditional themes, not directed at any individual, yet by 1612 it was claimed that 'certayne lewd Jigges songes and daunces vsed and accustomed at the play-house called the Fortune' attracted great crowds and caused distur-bance of the peace. The reason was that the jig had developed beyond rustic themes to satire on individuals; for although Baskervill does not question that many jigs were bawdy, yet, as C.J. Sisson wrote, bawdiness was not itself an issue at this period and he asks 'why should disreputable people throng to a theatre, after the main play, to hear and see a concluding song and dance? Why should such shows cause such tumults?' The answer Sisson gives is that the jig had turned to satire and 'in its full development, was one more form of libel and defamation, turning to dramatic purposes such topical scandals as afforded material for an evening's mirth and were likely to lead to breaches of the peace by the persons offended and their sym-pathisers.'[18] The professional Fool, John Shank, was a leading satiric jig-maker. Baskervill concludes from the following rhyme that Shank's reputation dwindled once his performances were curtailed:

> That's the fat foole of the Curtain, [William Rowley]
>   and the leane foole of the Bull: [Thomas Greene]
> Since Shank did leaue to sing his rhymes,
>   he is counted but a gull.   [Baskervill, pp.118-19]

The Curtain and the Bull were both popular theatres, which often successfully defied the authorities.

The example C.J. Sisson gives was the result of long-standing enmity between a pillar of society and the local people round Wells. It is interesting that the ribald accusations of adultery (which may or may not have been true) were provoked by the same man's attempt to prevent the more harmless entertain-ment of a Morris for a churchale. And so the satiric jig was part of the growing doctrinal polarization, where the Fool was neither the innocent, or the artificial of the old order, but a symbol of that order and so rejected by the Reformers. The pattern can be found in some Morality plays. In William Wager's *The longer thou livest the more Fool thou art* (1569) the Fool, Moros, is used to demonstrate the dangers of electing 'a popishe foole/To sit in a wise man's seate'.[19] Wager's Fool is irredeemable and it does not matter whether he is innocent or artificial. While Wager can accept him as a Fool, the Fool is not to be believed wiser than Solomon.[20] In 1569 Stephen Batman published *A Christall Glasse*, which follows medieval tradition by associating the Fool with the devil. It is interesting to note, however, that the leading folly is Avarice and not Pride. The change reflects the increasing acquisitiveness in the sixteenth century. Richard Day's 1578 *Booke of Christian Prayers*—known as Queen Elizabeth's Prayer Book—contains illustrations of Fools confronting Death. The man struggles while the woman, like the girl in Bergman's *The Seventh Seal*, follows obediently. Both man and woman wear the Fool's dress. The implication is that all inherit Adam's folly and frailty. In this, the Prayer Book goes back beyond distinctions between natural and artifical to a universal position.

Once theological law omitted the distinction it is easy to see how the artificial Fool might provide a more congenial house companion. But the temptations arising from being 'all-licensed' could be irresistible, and I suspect that the following attack by Thomas Lodge, in which the Fool is again equated with the devil, was due more to the discomforts others endured from the liberties taken than to any moral conviction. Lodge wrote, about 1596:

> Giue him a little wine in his head, he is cõtinually flearing and making of mouthes: he laughs intemperately at euery little occasion, and dances about the house, leaps ouer tables, out-skips mens heads, trips up his companions heeles, burnes sacke with a candle, and hath all the feats of a Lord of Misrule in the countrie.[21]

The description anticipates the arrival of James I of England's Fool, Archie Armstrong, who was one of the most boisterous and impudent Fools in court. However, he was granted a pension in 1611 and was given the freedom of the City of Aberdeen in 1617. His greatest enemy was Archbishop Laud, and Archie is famous for the prayer 'Great praise be given to God and little laud to the devil'. In 1637 he over-reached himself through interfering with Laud's church policy in Scotland. Archie's coat was pulled over his ears and he was kicked out of court. Not even that silenced him. Archie could be seen about London, dressed in clerical black, and when asked why he was not in his usual coat replied, 'O, my Lord of Canterbury hath taken it', for his own use.

Finally, the costuming of these Fools, jesters and clowns shows an interesting pattern. It is clear from the Inventories at St John's College, that the Fool's coat was parti-coloured. Bishop Ponet's remark on playing the Fool at Oxford shows that a checkered coat was part of the official regalia, and the Kingston records and Henry's 1510/11 Mask support the same conclusion. Further, Phillip Stubbes attacks the gay dress of the seasonal Fool and, similarly, Lord Tapp's fairground regalia continued in the same tradition. However, household and theatrical Fools did not always wear this. Somers, Tarlton and Kemp are all shown in other dress—often the rustic clown's— although Somers had Fool's coats for special occasions. In court, parti-colours seem to have been reserved for festivities and some formal receptions. The Morris Fool continued with medieval tradition, but the only playwrights who consistently used the gay dress were Morality writers. There were two reasons for this. Firstly, as T.W. Craik says, when acting troups were small and doubling a necessity, it was important that costumes were distinct from each other. The second reason was inherited from Peraldus: bright colours reflected inner Pride. Plays in which this is explicit are John Redford's *Wit and Science* (1531-47) in which Wit, fallen from Reson through his Pride finds himself in:

> Ingnorance cote hoode eares ye by the masse
> kokscome & all I lak but a bable,   [Farmer, ed. fol.23r.]

and Flatterie, in Lyndsay's *Satyre,* who draws attention to his dress, satanic loyalties and seasonal licence. In Wager's political Morality, Moros dresses in the Fool's coat at the end, where he rides happily to Hell on the devil's back.

Use of the Fool's coat is made in some romance comedies in which moral meaning is less overt. However, it is there in a lesser degree. In Anthony Munday's *John a Kent and John a Cumber (c* 1590) the evil influence of John a Cumber is tricked into defeat and his fall is marked by his being swept up into a

Morris dance as their Fool.

> Turnop [a clown]
> . . . our Morris lacks a folle, and we knowe none fitter for it than you M^r
> John heeres a coat spick and span new, it neuer came on any mans back
> since it was made, therefore . . . we are contented to account ye
> as our foole for euer hereafter.[22]

Cumber is a magician of note and it is only this disgrace which
shames him into accepting defeat. In this case the romance
battle is won by exposing not expelling the Fool. At about the
same period (1591/6) Lord Strange's Men presented Robert
Greene's play, *Frier Bacon and Frier Bongay* at the Rose theatre.
The moral in the romance sub-plot is explicit. Ralph, the King's
jester, wears Fool's dress and while Prince Edward is distracted
by dishonourable love Ralph makes the point that he and the
Prince should rightly change clothes. And while Edward
pursues his illicit passions, he gives Ralph the Prince's insignia
and lets him loose as a Lord of Misrule, while Edward conceals
his own identity. As a result the figure of folly enacts Edward's
interior folly. However, in *Mucedorus (c* 1595)—a play famous
for the stage direction later borrowed by Shakespeare 'exit
pursued by a bear'; and the play itself survived in rough form as
a folk play—Mouse, who plays a similar role to that of Ralph,
appears initially as a rustic clown. And the plays of Shakespeare
are enigmatic over the question of the Fool's dress. Touchstone
opens as a comic interpolater, but develops into a character
whose wit is the envy of Jacques. There has been considerable
discussion as to whether or not the part was begun with Kemp
in mind and then adapted for Robert Armin. Touchstone's
dress is described as 'motley' which covers a multitude of
possibilities. The only sure fact is that the dress caused Jacques
to expect a Fool of the kind described by Lodge, but instead
found a wit. Feste in *Twelfth Night,* is equally complex. In the
dramatis personae he is called 'clown'; his character is that of witty
Fool, yet the gaskins he wears do not bring parti-coloured tunic
and hose to mind. It would seem that he wore conventional
dress. Finally, the Fool in *King Lear* would be dressed appropriately in the long coats of the innocent, but no information is
given. So, none of these rare wise representations of the Fool in

England can be said definitely to have worn the gay costume of the artificial. It is possible that Shakespeare wished to avoid any satanic connections. However, it was the gay dress which was to survive in fairs as the dress of the English Fool.

At the turn of the seventeenth century the satirical, solo Fool was becoming a distinct figure in English society and, at the same time we have the brief climax of the witty and wise Fool of Erasmus' ancestry in the work of Shakespeare and Robert Armin. But, Armin himself did not forget he was Tarlton's heir. In *The Italian Taylor* (1606) he refers to his own playing of Dogberry: ' . . . pardon I pray you for the boldness of a Beggar, who hath been writ downe for an Asse in his time'.[23] In his own play, *Two maids of Moreclacke (c* 1599), Armin reveals a concern for controlling the Fool's behaviour on stage. In the play is a natural, Blue John—a well-known London innocent—, played by Armin at the first performance. The second is the witty Fool, Tutch. Neither character takes liberties with the action, as Kemp would have done, and Armin was careful to write out all the lines for both characters. Felver believes that Tutch began the change from irresponsible clown to witty Fool in Shakespeare's own plays (p.16). The first Quarto of *Hamlet,* written when the memory of Kemp was still fresh, contains a fuller rejection of improvisation than is found in the Folio:

And then you have some agen, that keeps one sute of ieasts, as a man is known by one sute of Apparell, and Gentlemen quotes his ieasts downe In their tables before they come to the play, as thus: Cannot you stay till I eat my porrige? and you owe me a quarters wages: and my coat wants a cullison: And your beer is sowre: and blabbering with his lips, And thus keeping in his cinkapase of ieasts, When God knows, the warme Clowne cannot make a ieast Unless by chance, as the blind man catcheth a hare. [fol. F.2.r.]

However, out of all the strands of sixteenth-century fooling it was to be the 'warme clowne' with a sharpened satirical wit who was to survive. The model can be seen in Archie Armstrong, whose last words to the court were 'Whea's Feule now?'. For once the talent needed to make the wise Fool a telling character passed with the close of Shakespeare's and Armin's careers, clowning and rough fooling once more became the popular attributes of the Fool. In the difficult years of the seventeenth century it was to be the tumbling, jig-making and satirical Fool, with his grimaces, dances and comments on the times who survived to earn his bread. The name of the Fool was to undergo a change, but as the example of Lord Tapp shows, the distinctive coat inherited from the fourteenth century moved with the Fool into the fairgrounds of the seventeenth century.

CHAPTER 4

Jack Pudding

In the seventeenth century a simple problem arose with regard to the man in cap and bell. While Parliament and Royalist parties both used the term 'fool' for each other's incapacities, the Fool *per se* needed to clarify his identity. Also, after 1642 the theatres were officially closed down, though many continued with surreptitious performances. But dramatists, unable to practise their craft openly, saw the follies of the stage upstaged by those of the world and were themselves instrumental in inverting the concept of folly: completing Armin's suggestion that all but the Fool were fools. A good illustration is the doggerel by Thomas Jordan who, in 1642, drew a picture of the world from the idiot's point of view and the idiot was no longer a protected natural, but an inmate of the lunatic asylum of Bedlam:

> The world is all but madness
> Then why are we confined
> To live by law, and lie in straw
> With hungar almost pined . . .
>
> Take my locks take my bolts off,
> Wee'le be as free as they be,
> Who keep such state, that none dare prate
> Yet are as mad as may be.   [BM MS E.246(6)]

Likewise, the artifical Fool appears in inverted form in *The Committee-Man Curried* (1647). Fools' liberty of speech, along with their disorderly role, are assigned to those who have silenced him:

> . . . since the prudent now have ordered so
> Fooles onely speake Cum Privilego
> We in obedience, so we can,
> Have given words to a Committee-man.   [BM MS E.398(21)]

Both types of the traditional Fool were estranged from society and because of the varying metaphoric use of his name, the identity of the man in cap and bell was no longer covered by the obvious name. But instead of disappearing into the pool of history, as first appears, the entertaining Fool kept his coat and changed his name. Three names appear most frequently and by the end of the eighteenth century were interchangeable: Zany—the Italian equivalent of Johnny—, Merry Andrew and Jack Pudding. Speaight and Baskervill show the names deriving from jigs performed by clowns but Willson Disher's illustration of seventeenth-century, fairground Fools shows that, originally, Merry Andrew, Jack Pudding and also the Antick were different characters. It is clear that initially Jack Pudding was the name for the English artificial Fool, which is not surprising since this fool had existed before the jig and his seasonal behaviour at Shrovetide in particular had much to do with puddings.

Illuminations to Psalm 13 frequently showed the Fool carrying a round shape. If not the globe of the earth it was a bladder-football, bread, cake or pudding. The edible varieties provided a visual metaphor for the line 'they eat up my people and their bread', and also pudding was the staple diet of many sections of society. Sayings abound: 'pudding time' was a time looked forward to whereas a 'pudding prick' was something worthless. But Thomas Bastard thought the subject fit for two humorous epigrams (Book 3, nos. 12 and 13). The earliest connections between man and the food were pejorative. Dunbar's 'Satire of Edinburgh' (*c* 1504) accuses the people of turning from moral behaviour to the pudding of Jock and James and the antics of the clown.[1] When Barclay contrasted the sports of country and court, he shows the presence of Fools in court—in both moral and literal senses—but does not even mention Fool, clown or pudding in the country where they originated from. It was the second half of the sixteenth century which saw the beginnings of 'pudding' name-calling and the timing coincides with the growing acceptability of Fools and also with the development of satiric writing. In Gabriel Harvey's splendid, splenetic attack on railers, he rants and rails himself and calls his opponents 'the bag-pudding of fooles'.[2]

Peele's play, *The old wives tale,* contains a character called
Corebus—the word defined in 1523 as 'a fool, deaf to
admonition'.[3] Corebus possesses a pudding and protests that it
is in danger of being stolen from him. 'Father do you see this
man? you little think he'll run a mile or two for such a cake, or
pass for a pudding. I tell you, father, he has kept such a begging
of me for a piece of this cake.'[4] Shakespeare, in *Measure for
Measure,* speaks of one imprisoned man as 'young Drop-heir
that killed lusty Pudding' (IV,iii,15), and Nashe, in 1589,
attacked Martin-Marprelate through May-game and pudding
analogy. 'Martin is the Mayde-marion . . . Wiggenton daunces
round about him in a Cotten-coate, to court him with a
Leathern pudding and a wooden ladle.'[5] 'Pudding' is the word
Nashe chose to describe the pig's bladder at the end of the
Fool's staff. The picture he paints for his political ends is itself
based on Fool-wooing games, such as those found in the Betley
window and Lyndsay's *Cupar Banns*; and the interesting thing is
that from the inception of the use of the term, satire, either
of or from the Pudding, is integral.

According to Speaight, Merry Andrews and Jack Puddings
alike dressed in either 'the rough clobber of the yokel [or]
sometimes in the motley of the fool' (p.27). However, the
evidence makes clear that until the mid-eighteenth century, the
one in Fool's dress was Jack Pudding. Willson Disher's fairground illustration gives one example. It is the 'Iacke Foole to a
Play' in parti-colouring and hood. And when, in 1680, Samuel
Butler came to write his satiric definitions of contemporary
types he even takes the Pudding's existence for granted and
only uses him as a comparison with the Mountebank and
Buffoon. The Buffoon was

> a tavern Terrae-filius, a Pudding impropriate without cure [care] of
> puppets. He pretends to the long-robe a fool's coat, and enjoys the
> privileges of it, to say what he pleases. He stains his impudence with
> scurrility, and a very little wit.   [Characters, p. 254]

The long Fool's dress suggests that Butler remembered the
common protective covering for the witless man. But Butler
dresses his Mountebank Pudding in the more practical coat and
a Fool's cap. He finds very little difference between the

Mountebank and his Pudding but

> his *Pudding* is his setter on. A Velvet Jerkin is his prime qualification, by
> which he is distinguished from his *Pudding*, as *He* is with his *Cap* from
> him.   [p.181]

In practice, roles between the two could merge and even be
reversed. One drawing shows the Pudding in the more elaborate periwig; and Joe Haines, who invites detailed study later,
was a low-comedian easily described by either name.

Joseph Addison is explicit in naming the parti-coloured Fool,
Jack Pudding. In the first year of the *Spectator*, 24 April, 1711, he
wrote:

> I must observe, that there is a set of Merry Drolls whom the Common
> People of all Countries admire, and seem to love so well, *that they could eat
> them* . . . I mean those circumforaneous Wits whom every Nation calls by
> the . . . Dish of Meat which it loves best. In Holland they are termed *Pickled
> Herrings*; in France *Jean Pottages;* in Italy, *Maccaronies;* and in Great Britain,
> *Jack Puddings*. These Merry Wags . . . always appear in a Fool's Coat and
> commit such blunders and Mistakes . . . as those who listen to them would
> be ashamed of.

The transference from the name, Fool, to Jack Pudding can
be traced in seventeenth-century writings. One good example is
in John Kirke's *Seven Champions of Christendome*, which was first
printed in 1638 and as a play it was either an extension of
already practised mumming drama, or was later added to play
acting in rural areas.[6] The play contains a Fool called clown and
who is, in Vice tradition, son of the devil, Tarpax. However,
when the clown speaks of his pleasure in accompanying St
George to earth, he declares an anticipation related more to
fairground shows than to the frustrating of the Saint's purpose:
'I doe love those things a life i'faith. Have you any squibs in
your country? and Green-men in your shows, and whizzers on
lines, Iacke Puddings upon Rope' [Fol.H.1.v]. Depending on
the point of view of the writer, Fool and Jack Pudding were
interchangeable, whether referring to Fools of Morris dance,
fairground or theatre, In 1654 Edmund Gayton compared
Sancho Panza's reaction to good news with the behaviour of a
Morris dance Fool. 'Sancho leaped at the word (above the rise

of Jack Pudding in a Morrice dance)'.[7] Morris dancers were
arrested in Staffordshire in 1655 and one Richard Floyd was
accused of 'acting the fool's part and profanely cursing others
with the plague',[8] and an earlier Fool recusant (1626) was
charged with being a Fool and wearing a Fool's coat'.[9] Then
when the Salisbury theatre was raided on 6 October 1647, Tim
Reade 'the foole' was taken away. There is no record of Andrew
Cane 'the clown of the Bull' being arrested and he was later
remembered as the 'perfect Jack Pudding'.[10] The Bull, the
Salisbury, the Cockpit and the Fortune were all raided on 1
January 1648—immediately prior to Charles I's execution. The
Fortune dispersed its audience and left 'Jack Pudding dancing
on the Ropes'.[11] And we return to the term 'fool' in Charles'
last entertainment at Witney in 1646, where a riotous debauch took
place under the title of 'Masque'. However, in the narrative
description, there is indication of the separate nature of Fools'
entertaining and that of the Morris dance itself. While the
dance was decorative and lively, it reflects more formally
against the behaviour of the Fools. The set dance was a beribboned clog dance and the Fools' tumbling appears to have been
a separate piece of improvisation. It is possible that the gallants,
too, joined in until they 'wearied both the Morris-Dancers, and
themselves with this sport'. Verses, which the author includes
at the end, are fairly long, but give the spirit and vigour of the
entertainment:

> With a noyse and a din
> Comes the Morris-dancer in
> With a fine linen shirt;
> But a buckram skinne.
> O! he treads out such a peale,
> From his paire of legs of Veale . . .
>
> Nor doe those knaves environ
> Their toes with so much iron
> Twill ruin a Smith to shoe him.
>
> I and then he flings about
> His sweate, and his Clout,
> The wersest thinke it too ells: [the size of clout or handkerchief]
> While the Yeeman [squire] thinke it meet
> That he jangle at his feete,

> The forhorse right eare jewells [the bells buckled on their calves]
> Then the Fool with his bawble fell
> to severall sports and to tumbling.   [BM MS E.336(14)]

And the final use of 'fool' instead of Jack Pudding appears to have been in 1680, when the High Tory was satirized as playing the Pope's game as Fool 'in a long gown' dancing in the Pope's Morris.[12] However, by this time the name Jack Pudding had all but supplanted that of Fool. Jack Pudding's eminence in fairgrounds was specific by 1647 when the attempted suppression of Bartholomew Fair was preempted by a proclamation opening it twelve hours before the Mayor of London arrived to ban it. The ballad recounting the Mayor's frustration leaves the final comment to Jack Pudding:

> On top of booth sat pudding John
> (Lord would be loath to sit thereon).
> I'me sure he wisht his Lordship gone,
>   Yet durst not tell him so.
> And when his Lordship left the Fayre,
> John set up throat did rend the Ayre,
> And glad he was, lowd did sweare,
>   he was gone.   [Morley, p. 183]

Swearing and rending the air with his voice convey the rough behaviour of the Kemp-like clown and the popularity of this type of Fool is recorded in *The Actors' Remonstrance* immediately after the official closure of the theatres in 1642. 'Our fooles, who had want to allure and excite laughter with their very countenances, at their first appearance on the stage . . . are enforced . . . to maintaine themselves by virtue of their bables' (BM MS E.86(6)). Jack Pudding dancing on the ropes at the Fortune theatre corresponds with Sir Aston Cockayne's lamentation on the falling standard of Fool dialogue in many theatres and suggests that a rougher standard—that of the fairground itself—had caught on at the popular theatres, such as the Bull, Fortune and Salisbury. Cockayne put this explicitly in 1653 in his Preface to the complete edition of Brome's plays. Cockayne looks forward to a future where:

> Our theatres of lower note in those

More happy daies, shall scorn the rustic Prose
Of a *Jack Pudding*.

The rustic, country clown, known as Jack Pudding, had
supplanted a refined Fool, such as Shakespeare had encouraged. And this was partly on account of audience taste. No
longer supported by a sophisticated court, theatre companies
sometimes had to abandon attempts to play serious drama even
when the authorities turned a blind eye. About Shrove Tuesday, 1654, a group of players attempted *Tamburlaine* and were
forced by their spectators 'to undresse and put off their Tragick
habits, and conclude the day with the merry milk-maids. And
unlesse this were done, and the popular humour satisfied . . .
the Benches, the tiles, the laths, the stones, Oranges, Apples,
Nuts, flew about most liberally'.[13] Bentley calls farcical pieces,
such as *The Merry Milkmaids*, Drolls. They could be easily
assembled and, if the law approached, disbanded. After the
Restoration two editions of the most popular were printed and
the second edition of 1673 contains an assertion by Robert
Kirkman that these light farces had been played throughout the
interregnum by various travelling groups, in 'London at
Bartholomew Fair and in the Country fairs. In Halls and
Taverns, on several Mountebanks Stages at *Charing Cross,
Lincolns-Inn-Fields* . . . by several Strolling Players, Fools and
Fiddlers, and Mountebanks Zanies' (Elson, p. 268). In other
words there were various groups who travelled and for different
purposes had to attract an audience to earn their livings. The
most famous travelling actor was Robert Cox. Though not
called a Fool or Jack Pudding, he was frequently called upon to
act the part, since Fool characters led the action. Recognition of
Fool-kinship was seized upon by one simpleton in the audience:
'Natural Jack Adams of Clarkenwel seeing him with Bread and
Butter on the stage and knowing him, cryed out, Cuz, Cuz, give
me some, give me some; to the great pleasure of the audience'
(Elson, p. 268). The meaning of 'droll' itself gradually shifted
from the piece played to the leading comic actor, until
Johnson's *Dictionary* finalised the change, giving as the primary
definition of *droll* 'Jester; a buffoon, a jackpudding'. According
to Kirkman, the Drolls were the plays themselves and, as can be
imagined, much interchange of ideas and actors took place

before the Restoration. Mention of Zanies, which is the Italian for Johnny, introduces the question of influence from Italy and whether or not Harlequin took over from the English Fool to the extent that the latter disappeared. The question is often over-simplified. It is generally thought that while the English Renaissance was at its height *Commedia Dell'Arte* farces could not compare in variety and vitality and it was only by about 1680 that English plays had deteriorated to the point where continental performers introduced by Charles II completely ousted the style of English humour. But, as already shown, English Fools were already popular if they were as grotesque and farcical as the Italian and the confusion in style led to a confusion in name until about 1700. In the fairgrounds, where Jack Pudding thrived, Harlequin enjoyed a comparable and complementary popularity. 'Zany' for Fool was current usage by 1637 when D'Avenant's Masque, *Brittania Triumphans*, contained an anti-masque of:

> A mountebank in the habit of a grave doctor
> A zany
> A harlekin
> An old lame charwoman
> Two pale wenches presenting their urinals, and he
> distributing his receipt out of a budget.[14]

Here, there seems to have been an early attempt to parody the Italian *mountebanc* and his entertainers. However, the mountebank has had an unnecessarily bad press and this has still not received adequate redress. I agree with E.S. de Beer who, in his annotated edition of John Evelyn's *Diary*, expresses the opinion that the Venetian *montebanc* was an offshoot of *Commedia Dell'Arte* and that like other strolling performers his income came from the entertainment he gave rather than from the deceitful sale of noxious chemicals. John Evelyn's own account shows this to have been the case, and at the same time reveals an idiosyncratic attitude towards these chemicals and the hope that they would cure as well as entertain. When, in 1681, Evelyn attended a demonstration of the properties of phosphorous at the Royal Society, the experiment made in good faith by Dr Sleare simply reminded Evelyn of a previous demonstration seen in Italy. 'This noble experiment, exceeded all that I ever had seen of this nature, unlesse that which I accidentally beheld . . . a certain *Mountebank* at Rome.'[15] Evelyn went on to say that while other *ciarlatini*[16] required monkeys and Jack Puddings to attract crowds, the man with the self-igniting chemical needed no such outside assistance to obtain money. Further, Evelyn claims healing properties for Dr Sleare's work; a claim not made by Dr Sleare in his own written account of the experiment.[17] Therefore, it would seem that the public itself contributed to any accidents and the evidence surrounding the travelling English mountebank all suggests that entertainment was the primary source of income. For example the saying went:

> A mountebank without his fool
> Is in a sorrowful case.   [Strutt, p. 236]

In 1682 a decree was made which compelled all applications for licences to perform as mountebanks to be made to Thomas Killigrew (self-proclaimed jester to Charles II) instead of by proxy to Mr John Clarke, bookseller. This may indeed have given 'jurisdiction over all the Merry Andrews and Jack-Puddings in every Fair throughout England' (Morley, p. 221) into Killigrew's hands, but since Killigrew was Master of the Revels the decree also affirms that the authorities considered mountebank doctors and their associates as strolling players and this continued until about 1800. The last named Master of Revels to have 'power of collecting even half-crowns from Merry Andrews and Jack-Puddings of every country fair all over England' was John Charles Crowle, who died about 1805.[18]

Satire was the entertainment offered and, in a country where news outside the cities was scarce, it would not be surprising if satirical newsvendors and their tumblers were received kindly and until the mid-eighteenth century it appears that they enjoyed more success than groups of genuine strolling actors. In 1712 the *Spectator* reported that a poverty-stricken group of strollers performing from a cart attempted Vanbrugh's elaborate comedy, *The Relapse*. The grandiose Lord Foppington was reduced to the necessity of wearing the Fool's parti-

coloured hose as the only indication of his role.[19] In the same
period Thomas Marchant recorded the social welcome given to
the mountebank and his companions. In January 1718 he
recorded in his Diary that:

> A mountebank came to our toune to-day. He calls himself Dr. Richard
> Harness. Mr. Scutt and I dranke with the tumbler. Of his tricks I am no
> judge; but he appears to me to play well on the fiddle.
>
> Feb. 7th. The mountebank still here. I spent 4d with my cousin Lindfield.

Marchant doesen't say he *bought* from the visitor, but in the
above notes mentions only the entertainment value. And again
on 5 May 1721 he wrote: 'A mountebank's man here the 2nd
time. He says his name is William Luby. I agreed to keep a
horse for him at 2s per week. I drank with him yesterday at the
Swan'.[20] The travellers were not only welcome but could pay
their way. This was not surprising if satire and clowning were
dexterously done for, by 1731 there were about two thousand
fairs held in England from January to November—most of
which lasted at least a week.[21] An able entertainer who relied on
verbal wit and a small group of inventive performers had more
chance of earning a living than a group of strolling actors who
needed more expensive properties to give an adequate performance. Later in the century the situation changed. *The
Connosseur* recorded on 4 July 1754 that a company of strollers in
the West Country was a more attractive proposition for the
mountebank's Fool already playing in the same town. The
strollers 'finding the Doctor's *Zany* a droll fellow, decoyed him
into their service'.

As Butler said, mountebanks were frequently indistinguishable from their Jack Puddings, and history shows that a
Harlequin was often an addition, as a confederate of the
Pudding and not his rival. The combination caused initial
confusion over the identity of Harlequin when he became
popular in the London-based, licensed theatres. A Harlequin
one day could be either a Jack Pudding or Mountebank the
next. For example Joe Haines turned mountebank after playing
Harlequin in Ravenscroft's *Scaramouche a Philosopher* (1677).
Earlier confusion shows in John Walker's 1648 *History of Inde-*

pendence, where he attempts to divert possible disapproval through fairground analogy. 'I advise thee not to apply what I say to the *Parliament or Army in generall* . . . No, it is the *Grandees, Junto-men,* the *Hocus-Pocuses,* the State Mountebanks, with their *Zanies* and *Jack-Puddings*' (fols. A2, r & v). Even after the Restoration, when the Italian characters had become popular at court and in those theatres the court patronized, many in the audience still could not distinguish between the Italian and the English Fool. After some random name-calling the confusion of identity was finally put into words and thereby clarified by the Harlequin of William Mountfort's *Life and death of Dr. Faustus made into a farce*[22] (1686). Whereas Edward Howard in *The Woman's Conquest,* Edward Ravenscroft in *Scaramouche a Philospher* and Aphra Behn in *The Emperor in the Moon* were content to use Jack Puddings and Harlequins indiscriminately within a mountebank context, Mountfort used the plot of Scaramouche dressing as the legitimate Dr Faustus and frightening Harlequin into the following confession:

> I am poor *Harlequin*: By the Learned I am called *Zane,* by the Vulgar *Jack Pudding.* I was late Fool to a Mountebank, and last night . . . I eat up a Pot of *Bolus* instead of Hasty Pudding . . . for which my Master has turned me out of Doors. [p. 8]

Many successful comedies used the potential of the mountebank and his Fool servants as the basis for all or some of the plot until well into the eighteenth century and this indicates the familiarity of many sections of society with the original. Any travelling mountebank needed for success at least two Fools: one a Harlequin and the other a Jack Pudding. Only one collection of speeches remains and the Frontispiece shows a Harlequin pointing to the Doctor, which has been taken as an example of Harlequin's usurpation of the English Fool. However, the Preface places Jack Pudding's antics within the show: like the jig a coda and advertisement. The Pudding's forte lay in clownish acrobatics on the ropes. He 'mounted his hempen Fortune flying like a Bird in the Air and when he has fool'd it about half an Hour he promises his mobbish Spectators more Diversions the next visit'.[23] Ned Ward in *The London Spy (c* 1690) records a 'Prodigally Pert *Jack Pudding* . . . Ridiculing an *Italian*

Sonetta in the Balcony, to draw People into the *Booth*' (p. 101). We do not know whether the booth performance was play or speech; however Jack Pudding imitating an Italian singer demonstrates the interplay between traditions.

Satire plays a large part in the speeches in the collection. We can see too how ambivalent the relationship between Doctor and Fool was, as Samuel Butler said. The most sophisticated speech is one which was performed by the FOOL on behalf of his patron, the High German Doctor, gifted in all languages save that of the country he is in. The cures have nothing to do with medicine but eveything to do with political upheavals. In *sottie* manner, the Fool claims the Doctor

> has cur'd twelve Foreign Ministers of State of those twin Plagues, Bribery and Infidelity; Six Kings of a Tyrannical Fevers; the whole Conclave of Cardinals of Pride, Laziness and Hypocrisy; and the present Pope of the Antichristian Evil.   [p. 8]

The last line brings the year 1687 to mind, when change of religion in England did officially cure the Pope of the evils he had been charged with. Other illnesses related to this, and the Vicar of Bray attitude adopted for survival are promised cure through *Mollifying Ointment* 'for the suppling and stretching of narrow and hide-bound Consciences, extraordinary useful for all fashionable Zealots, who are desirous of making their Religion subservient to their interest'. Applied every Saturday night the patient may go to church Sunday morning, to Meeting Sunday afternoon and 'return home as devout Hypocrites as if they had never gone at all'. Finally, *Orvietano* is claimed to be preventative medicine against all forms of religious or political disillusionment. 'It expels all Low-Country Schism by a Belch; carries off all Disloyalty in a Fart; and is the best Restorative to strengethen weak Faith, and decay'd Allegiance, that ever was discover'd since the Fall of Adam'. The speaker, a self-styled 'English Fool', gives a piece of pure political satire and makes absurd any idea that the speech was intended to dupe onlookers into buying the products as anything other than humorous mementoes—tickets to hearing the latest satirical news. Thomas Marchant's diary a few years later gives a similar implication. Fourpence was spent hearing the mountebank, not in payment for his products. It is just this entertainment value which is emphasized in the exploits of Joe Haines around the country.

To my mind, Haines was born out of his time. As Willson Disher points out, comedians in the 1680s found their place in society unsatisfying since the nobility 'wanted to see themselves raised to the sublimely heroic, above the ridicule of the clown . . . The Elizabethan clown may have been a serving man, but he was a serving-man sitting in his lord's chair. The fool of the Restoration was a whipping-stock for the gallants' (p. 72). Haines was frequently in trouble. His sense of the absurd continually gave offence. He went to France to learn dancing and was imprisoned for impersonating an English Peer. On release he returned to England and in 1685 performed a 'satirical-political-topical'[24] droll in Bartholomew Fair, called *The whore of Babylon, the devil and the Pope.* Considering that the year was that of James II's accession it is not surprising that Haines was once more arrested and only escaped second imprisonment by the subtle pleading that 'he did it in respect of his Holiness; for, whereas many ignorant people believed the Pope to be a beast, he showed him to be a fine, comely old gentleman' (Disher, pp. 75-6). Report continues that when bailiffs arrived the following morning to collect a twenty-pound fine, Joe responded by greeting the first man passing in a coach as his brother. The man, who happened to be the Bishop of Ely, was so embarrassed that he agreed to pay the fine. (Daniel, p. 7) Haines' career in the London theatres was equally irregular. As already mentioned he performed Harlequin with great success at the King's theatre in the first major Harlequin play, *Scaramouche a Philosopher,* by Edward Ravenscroft in 1677. In the subsequent production, *Cataline's Conspiracy,* the tragic lead was taken by Charles Hart, and Haines was reduced to a walk-on part as one of the Senators. As an expression of his annoyance Haines

put on a Scaramouche dress, a large full ruff, whiskers from ear to ear, and a long Merry-Andrew's cap [Disher's term]. With a short pipe in his mouth and a little three legged stool in his hand, he followed Hart on the

stage, set himself down behind him, and began to smoke his pipe, laugh
and point at him. Hart, whose 'exactness and grandeur' were upset, turned
him out of doors.   [p. 76]

Haines transferred briefly to the Duke's Company, where he
had a second success in Ravenscroft's farce, *Mamamouchi*,
despite its being considered 'a Foolish Play' by the critics.[25]
Chronology suggests that it was after this that Haines first set
out for the continent. However, the contemporary biographer,
Tobias Thomas saw nothing malicious in Haines' behaviour,
only jokes. 'Plain *Jo Hayns*, the learned *Dr. Hayns*, or even the
dignified *Count Hayns*, . . . his Disguises had more of the
Humourist than the Imposter in them [and] his Frauds were
rather to be call'd his Frolicks' (Preface). The humour was lost
on most of society; of Haines' own time and later on Lord
Macaulay. When writing of the Great Revolution of 1688, when
Protestantism was restored, Macauley also saw reason to berate
Haines for his hypocrisy:

> A still more famous apostate was Joseph Haines, whose name is now
> almost forgotten, but who was well-known in his own time as an
> adventurer of versatile parts, sharper, coiner, false witness, sham bail,
> dancing master, buffoon, poet, comedian. Some of his prologues and
> epilogues were much admired by his contemporaries: and his merit as an
> actor was universally acknowledged. However, this man professed himself
> a Roman Catholic, and went to Italy in the retinue of Castelmaine, but was
> soon dismissed for mis-conduct . . . Haines had the impudence to affirm
> that the Virgin Mary had appeared to him and called him to repentance.
> After the Revolution, he attempted to make his peace with the town by a
> penance more scandalous than the offence. One night, before he acted in a
> farce, he appeared on the stage in a white sheet with a torch in his hand,
> and recited some profane and indecent doggerel, which he called his
> recantation.[26]

Considering that in 1687 Haines published a satiric dialogue on
Dryden's religious reversals, it appears that Haines' own
behaviour was a parody of that of Dryden and many others.
However, it was not long after this that his fortunes continued
as the mountebank-Fool, Dr Haines. He 'took pains to organise
his retinue of Tumblers, Dancers &c., so that having eas'd the
town of some of its Rubbish he sets forward on his Journey to

Hartford' (Thomas, p. 35). There, he discovered another mountebank already established and known as the Unborn Doctor. The only way for Haines to gain his own recognition was to challenge the Unborn Doctor to a Faustian contest of powers.

Being both mounted on the public stage, and surrounded by a numerous auditory eager to hear this learned dispute, Joe desired that each might stand upon a joint stool. 'Gentlemen'. said Joe, 'I thank you for your good company, and hope soon to prove how grossly you have been deceived by this arch-imposter. I come hither . . . from performing many miraculous cures throughout Europe. I prognosticate some heavy judgement will fall on the head of that impudent quack. May the charlaton tumble ingloriously, while the true doctor remains unhurt'. At which words, Haynes's Merry-Andrew, who was underneath the stage, a cord fast to B—s stool . . . pulled it from under him. Joe was borne home in triumph and B— hooted out of the town. [Thomas pp. 37-8]

It's hard to ignore the mock sermon aspect of these speeches. The title 'doctor' combines pseudo-medicine with the medieval tradition of the *sermon joyeux*. Many pieces claim miraculous cures. It is likely that the phenomenon of ritual return from the dead was already part of folk play and so the basis of the mountebank's material would already have foundation in the games of the rural audiences.

One of the printed speeches is by Haines. Under the pseudonym of High German Doctor we find a pompous figure himself suffering from constipation of multi-syllabic words. Taken from the page, the monologue is less obviously satiric than the actor's own style of living, but in performance it may have given scope to Haines' power of impersonation. There is no doubt that many mountebanks relied on tricks and sleight-of-hand to attract their audiences but there is no evidence that the early performing doctors were the dangerous quacks they were later made out to be. Support for this comes from Strutt and R.W. Chambers, who, writing in the nineteenth century, lay their emphasis on the entertainment these provided. Corroboration comes from nineteenth-century terminology for hard-up circuses practising deceit to attract audiences. Such tricks as painting horses a thoroughbred colour were known as mountebanking. In the same period penurous strolling players at fairs were called 'mummers'. Both shifts in meaning draw attention to the cross-fertilization between fairground entertainers: the travelling player with holes in his stockings might well have both resembled the local mumming troup and appealed to the pockets of the audiences on similar grounds. Fred Karno recalled one hard winter in 1880, when some of the circus troup he was with blackened their faces and went singing for pennies in the midland mining towns.[27]

However, strollers, mountebanks and their Jack Puddings enjoyed a considerable period of prosperity. The tradition may have begun before 1600, though moral plays (even with Fools) performed by small travelling groups of the early 1500s cannot be compared with the farce and satire which began during the interregnum. And at the same time the Fool, having lost his moral approbrium and gained a tongue of his own, became the outspoken Jack Pudding still dressed in the garb of his ancestors. After 1660 numerous references to Jack Puddings at fairs can be found. In 1680 an anti-papal Droll compared the church of Rome to a fairground. The priest was 'Jack Pudden [who] makes the parade of the show': ie. he serves to draw the masses inside the church as Ned Ward observed Jack Pudding did for the booth (Morley, pp. 198-218). In 1693, well after the Great Revolution, a pro-Stuart Droll was enacted. In this Jack Pudding played 'Chorus' and extemporized on the events portrayed. This Droll proved so popular and increased in the length of performance and size of audience to such an extent that the actors were eventually jailed (Morley, p. 260). However, even Macaulay appreciated its Aristophanaic humour. It may well have been this Droll which prompted the vocabulary for one translation of Milton's *Defence of the People of England*— written in 1648 and revived in the 1690s to defend the second revolution. One translator interprets *stultus* (fool) as 'the extempore lines of some antic *jack pudding* [which] deserve printing better' than the words of the pro-Stuart writer. Even Jeremy Collier in his attack on the Profaneness of the English Stage translated verses by the Frenchman, Boileau, into Jack Pudding[28] terminology, though his banishment of the actors to Southwark tressles was a fate happily embraced by actors like

Haines and Shuter, since the latter was reported to have earned more in a month at Bartholomew Fair than during the rest of the year in the indoor, licensed theatres.[29]

CHAPTER 5

Later attitudes

It wasn't long before insulting comparisons grew up, using the term, Jack Pudding, where earlier 'fool' had been used. The most obvious was the derogatory reaction to some mounte-banks such as Hans Buling who came over to England about 1670. 'He was an odd figure of a man, and was extremely fantastical in his dress. He was attended by a monkey, which he had trained up to act the part of a jack-pudding; a part which he had formerly acted himself, and which was much more natural to him' (Granger, 6, p. 169). And in about 1675 George Villiers compared the wealthy aristocracy who impoverished them-selves to buy an army command to a Fool playing with a hobby-horse in folk play. Again 'Jack Pudding' is the term used.

> There's a *Fop Mortgages* all his land,
> To buy a gawdy *Play-thing*, a *Command*
> To ride a *Cock-horse*, were a Scarf at's Arse
> And play the *Pudding* in a *May-day Farce*.[1]

An interesting piece of tongue-in-cheek can be found in a letter of 1715 from a Fool turned away by his Mountebank Master at Bangor. In reference to his old occupation the writer calls himself Merry Andrew, while, now he is out of work, he is a Jack Pudding and the other title applies to the solo Doctor. You 'are turn'd now into a meer *Merry-Andrew*, like your old trusty Servant *Jack-Pudding*' who will, when the letter is completed send his '*Fools Coat* and Patch-work *Breeches*' to his one-time master.[2] Merry-Andrew looks like the more respectable name for the Jack Pudding occupation, though this is relative to the means of gaining that occupation. For the Doctor it is a come-down; and at the height of the Jack Pudding vogue, the name was not only used derogatively, but was brought in as satirical mouthpiece in various wars of words. The two which stand out are the theatrical war on stardards of comic writing and in battles between Whigs and Tories. The way the Fool is brought in illustrates the *sottie*-like articulateness which Jack Pudding had developed during the seventeenth century. The reasons for the satire were not unlike those of the earlier French satire: disillusionment with government, the church and also the importation of the rival continental comedy. The English Elizabethan concept of comedy had been that of a period of disorder within an ordered social framework. By 1666 Wycherley wrote 'where else but on stages do you see/Truth pleasing, or rewarded honesty', clearly implying that social norms were reversed and only lying Fools in the form of fawning servants suited high society, as Disher said. The Fool as such disappeared from plays after one or two attempts to reintroduce him. The first was in *Thorney Abbey* (thought to have been written during the interregnum and published in 1662). The Fool comes on before the play and protests at his omission from the play proper:

> they are all fools in the *Tragedy*; and you are fools that come to see the *Tragedy*; and the *Poet's* a fool who made the *Tragedy*, to tell a story of a King and a Court, and leave a *fool* out on't; when in *Pacy's* and *Somer's* and *Patche's* and *Archie's* times, my venerable Predecessours, a *fool* was always the *Principal Verb*.   [*Gratiae Theatrales*]

The Fool's despair is not that of a Cacurgus, banished in mid-winter. Instead of temporary banishment outside the playing season, all concept of season had gone and it is the theatre itself dispensing with the obvious mischief maker. And the fawning replacement who appears in Etheredge's *The Comical Revenge* (1664) to provoke intrigue is exposed as a Jack Pudding. Dr Michael Cordner notes that one short scene does nothing to further the action and only establishes that beneath the affected exterior of Dufoy lies a

> Jack Pudding to a Mountebank,
> And turn'd off for want of wit: my Master pick'd him,
> Up before a Puppit show, mumbling a halfpenny
> Custard.   [III, iv.]

And the protestation Dufoy makes in reply is that he only

happened to be there enjoying 'de Jack-Puddinge [that] did play a hundred pretty trike'. Whether or not the accusation was true is less important than the association between the master and servant, for in the last attempt to bring back the honest-speaking Elizabethan Fool, the Fool offers the concession of promising to behave like Dufoy, 'a fashionable Fool, learn to lisp, speak *French*, wear a Bag, and be very affected'. This was as late as 1744 in Thomas Odingsell's *The Prodigall* and the Fool was played by Charlotte Charke, Cibber's daughter. And her protestation that though the age is much inclined to be satirical, men can't stand the truth, is borne out when the Fool is very quickly borne out.

It is curious that the derision aimed at Dufoy includes the claim that he lacks wit; or that he is nearer to the simpleton than the witty satirist Jack Pudding usually was. Bearing in mind that the name came from the Fool of country game ancestry it is not so surprising that there was some overlap between the simpleton—now the 'cully' or 'cuddy'—and witty pudding. Samuel Butler kept the distinction between the two, but was himself hardest on the rustic. The innocent of earlier centuries was an aesthetic pariah, 'a centaur, a Mixture of Man and Beast, like a Monster engendered by unnatural copulation, a Crab grafted on an Apple . . . neither made by Art, nor Nature, but in Spight of both, by evil custom' (*Characters*, p. 130). The clown had both reclaimed his former stupidity and fallen to the nadir of educated opinion. John Gay mocked the cully who was impressed by 'Jack Pudding in his parti-coloured Jacket [who] Tosses the Glove and Jokes at every Packet'.[3] Low human behaviour in both Jack Pudding and spectator reach parity in Gay's earlier poem, 'The two Monkies' (1711) for it is the monkeys who express their amazement at the popularity with all sections of society, of men who behave like monkeys. Jack Pudding is a classic example.

> Two monkies went to Southwark fair,
> No critic had a fouler air:
> They forced their way through draggled folks
> Who gap'd to catch Jack-Pudding's jokes. [*Fables*, no. 40]

And in Peter Motteux' ballad, 'A description of Bartholomew fair' (1680), 'Iacke-Pudding' diverts the 'Country Cully', while the pickpocket eases the rustic visitor of his money. And links between the Pudding and his own clownish origins are recalled in various comments. George Daniel quotes an item written in Bartholomew fair's defence, when the authorities tried again to close it in 1701: 'Jack Pudding who grins wofully for a sake of his *namesake*; . . . why not be merry your *own way*, and let mountebanks be merry *theirs*?' Rosenfeld quotes a 1717 poem in which the established actor, Penkethman, saw no indignity in sitting dauntlessly 'In fam'd Grimace'.[4] And in the poem, 'The great Boobee', it is the cully who eventually discovers how to put his ignorance to use in London:

> If I can but a license get,
>   to play before the Bears . . .
> Then who dares call me Fool or Ass,
>   *or a great Boobee.*   [Ashton, p. 51]

Ironically, itinerant actors or strollers complained as early as 1701 that the incursion of mock simpleton Puddings at fairs was taking away their livelihood and not adding to it.

> Oh! mourn with us all you that live by play
> The *Reformation* took our gains away:
> We are as good as dead now money's gone,
> No *Droll* is suffer'd, not a single one.
> *Jack Pudding* now our grandeur doth exceed,
> And grinning granny is by fates decreed
> To laugh at us, and to our place succeed.[5]

Sixty years previously it had been the 'grinning granny' who was the object of pity, according to 'The Actors' Remonstrance', when forced into fairground Drolls by persecution of the legitimate theatre. Whether or not there was a further decline in standards is not easy to determine. It is more likely that the strolling players suffered from the successful combination of mountebank and Fool. For Addison's description of the Pudding—'the merry wag who commits blunders and mistakes'—implies that when playing on the ropes he would have to be as skilful as today's circus clowns: giving the appearance of incompetence while executing dangerous acts. On the other hand, there is the evidence for simpleton Jack Puddings, such as that given above, and constant associations between Jack Pudding and the Cully. Dr Leverigo sang with his Fool, Pinkanello, 'Jack Puddings for Cuddens', and George Daniel includes a more improbable story of a country fellow stopping on horseback to gape at Jack Pudding. We are asked to believe that his admiration was such that thieves stole his horse from under him without his noticing.[6] Whether or not such stories were true, the continued gulling of the simpleton by the clever Fool is an interesting point of contact between the Middle Ages and the stooge of the present-day comic duo.

In the licensed, or patented theatres, some writers adopted the rough, farcical element—even Congreve after his official retirement in 1700[7]—and others opposed it. Thomas Shadwell wrote in 1678-9 that to some people 'Wit signifies nothing in a Comedy; but the putting out of Candles, kicking down of Tables, falling over Joynt-stools impossible accidents and un-natural mistakes (which they absurdly call plot) are the poor things they rely on' (Preface, *A True Widoe*). Seven years earlier, Edward Howard had attempted his own restoration of comic values, and the elimination of perpetrators of 'unnatural mistakes' etc. His long Preface to *The woman's conquest* attempts to convince that comedy must 'entertain our passions, with delight', and what is merely horseplay is not truly comic. In a familiar metaphor he compares farce to the mule and comedy to the horse. There is kinship between the two but the mule is not only sterile but has has somewhat longer ears. Howard tried to undermine fashion in the first of three prologues by using farce to send up farce. As might be expected, this part contains more vigour than the rest of the play, with the result that the mule is the more interesting creature. Firstly Angel announces:

> Be it known to all here present, that we are to act a Farce today, that hath sixteen Mimicks in it, Severall Jack-Puddings and Punchinellos, never presented before, with two and thirty Dances and Jiggs *a-la-mode* besides.

A second character wishes all such characters back to their

tressle stages, but despite this the grinning granny enters 'tredoudling' with his hands and is greeted by Angel as 'the very Pudding of [the Farce] that must fill the Audience up to the throat with laughter'. (Connections with eating are rarely far away, particularly in the later satire.) In Howard's play, Ben Jonson turns in his grave when the Pudding begins his antic dance and frightens the first Prologue off the stage by appearing through the floorboards. Jonson has the stage to himself while he condemns all farces and then a third Prologue is spoken in which it is hoped that the audience will now have forgotten their taste for the degenerate comedy and will watch comedy as it should be written. It is unfortunate that the play which then follows is a wooden and derivative piece.

The most successful attacks on degenerate fooling, as they saw it, were made by Odingsell and Fielding. They held to the idea of satirizing farce throughout the plays written against it. Odingsell's *Bays Opera* (1730) not only gives a graphic display of the decline of serious theatre but places the English Fool, called Pantomime, above Harlequin, who serves as second in command. And the songs quite explicitly trace both the origins and the rise of the two characters from low social origins to their present authority as Father of Buffoons and Prime Minister:

> Stalls no more invite us,
> Scatter'd Pence requite us;
> While our mimic Postures Mobs admire.
> No more market Stages,
> No more Quacking Sages
> Shall, to vend their pills, our Jokes inspire.   [p. 4]

Instead, a complete reversal is enacted. Apollo, the god of the highest arts, is overthrown to descend to the status of strolling player himself. The supporters of Pantomime sing 'if you think fit./With your Physick and Wit,/Turn Quack or Comic Stroller'. In the same year Thomas Ralph wrote *Harlequin's Opera,* which was performed at Goodman's Fields and attempted a truce with the comic foreign invader. In the aftermath of battle it is decided that Harlequin will be the Doctor who plays Fool, sharing the profits with the rest. The suggestion inevitably provokes associations with the mumming Fool, who does just that. And agreement is only tentatively reached since a poet replies, 'this is only on condition the Doctor turns Stroller, and plays his Tricks only in Country Towns, and at yearly Fairs'; thereby returning Harlequin to his means of assimilation into English entertainment and of course, bringing back the usurped Apollo. Fielding tried, initially, to ignore the farce and write according to Restoration comedy techniques. His first admission of defeat came in 1729, when he allowed the publication of a revised piece, called *The Author's Farce*. In this the 'Luckless' author is besieged by scribblers and a Jack Pudding makes one entrance to announce this action and then exits with the mob. In 1736, after further attemps to ignore fashion, Fielding once more faced 'this French mongrill and apeing age' with his *Dramatick Satire on the Times; Pasquin*. One point of interest is the illustration in the Preface, which shows Harlequin and Clown, Harlequin's servant, ignored by the Queen of Common-sense, who pours money into Fielding's pocket. The conquest of Common-sense over the Queen of Ignorance happens ironically after the first Queen's death. Touches of Fielding at his best appear as the actress appears as the Ghost of Common-sense before the character had been killed. 'I ask Pardon, Sir, in the hurry of the Battle I forgot to come and kill myself'.

> *Fustian*: Well, let me wipe the Flower off your Face then . . . Go to the Corner of the Scene, and come in as if you had lost the Battle.

Eventually, in 1744, Fielding wrote the following piece of defiance: *Tumble-Down Dick or Phaeton in the Suds, interlarded with Burlesque, Grotesque, Comic Interludes called Harlequin a Pick-Pocket, Being ('tis hoped) the last Entertainment that will ever be Exhibited on any Stage*. Fielding's direct opinions against the degradation of the comic writer are found in the *Covent-Garden Journal* for 1752. 'Writers are not I presume to be considered as mere jack-puddings, whose business is only to excite laughter; this indeed, may sometimes be intermixed, and served up, with graver [pun on gravy] matters, in order to titillate the palate', (no. 10). Again, and as Neil Rhodes has shown with regards to earlier satiric writing, gastronomic associations are never far away from satire.[8] Jack Pudding has literal connections but it might have been this which made him such an appropriate spokesman. Before turning to the best of the Jack Pudding satires, I would like to pass through some of the mental contortions writers tried to defend their own opinions on farce. Butler, in his criticism of critics, changed his view from that in *Characters*. Opposing critics who wish everything to be judged by the standards of the ancients, he defends the witty Pudding against those who can only tolerate Fools who go out into storms with King Lears. Later, Charles Gildon sat on the fence to assess the conflict, and pointed out that if all irrational and absurd activity was banished from the stage, many say that Othello would be dismissed along with Jack Pudding. And the most ingenuous twist was devised by Anthony Collins in his *Discourse concerning ridicule and an irony in writing* (1729), where he ignores the presence of great British satirists of the time, such as Pope and Swift, to argue that satire or the 'buffooning rustick Air' is the only weapon of those deprived of freedom of expression by a tyranny. 'The higher the slavery, the more exquisite the Buffoonery [and] the greatest of *Buffoons* are the *Italians* . . . 'Tis the only manner in which the poor cramped Wretches can discharge a free Thought . . . what wonder is it if we, who have more Liberty, have less Dexterity in that egregious way of *Raillery* and *Ridicule*' (p. 25). Apart from the main hole in his argument, Collins himself goes on to satirize, for example, Quakers, whose attitude is that of 'a *Jack-Pudding, Merry Andrew* or Buffoon, with all the seeming Right, Authority, and Privilege, of the Member of some Established Church of abusing all the World but themselves' (p. 54).

Though the major English satirists took their lines of attack along original lines, there was a low-brow satirical conflict in pamphlets and journals which descended to fairground figures for their mouthpieces and butts. The most well-known writers are the Scotsmen, John Arbuthnot and Thomas Gordon, both of whom wrote pamphlets and contributed to the journal, *The Craftsman*. Arbuthnot, appropriately, a scientist with leanings towards medicine, as well as satirist. In his first pamphlets on

John Bull, begun about 1712, it appears that he coined the
name, John Bull, to cover rapacious politicians. The name of
course remained as a proud term for the Englishman. However,
with the death of Queen Anne there was a further struggle for
power and Arbuthnot commemmorated this in his Crown-Inn
pamphlets of 1713-14. Among the many mountebanks preaching for his right to possess Crown-Inn is one specific Merry
Andrew with 'a special knack at railing' (p. 30). In a Haines-
like manner he 'mounted the Stage, to a numerous Crowd of
Auditors and Spectators' and after his personal advertisement
he attacked the real doctor with such success that every one of
his 'pacquets' was purchased and the crowds carried him to his
lodgings 'with loud shouts of O rare *Andrew*!'. As his lodgings
were at Mitre-Inn, religious dispute in the running of Crown-
Inn, ie. the country, is implied. In 1726, the most famous of the
Pudding satires was written by either Arbuthnot or Thomas
Gordon. (A Glasgow edition of the complete works of John
Arbuthnot, 1751, includes this work without reservation.) This
satire appears with the apparently meaningless title of 'A
learned dissertation on Dumpling' or *The Dumpleid*. It is now
agreed that the defence of Pudding is a euphemistic metaphor
for the defence of lining one's pockets through the gaining of
power or close association with those in power: a practice
indulged in by both Whigs and Tories, but particularly by the
Duke of Marlborough during the continental wars. The history
of such pickings is traced through the long existence of the folk
Fool, Jack Pudding, whose mother invented such a fine
Pudding for King John that Jack rose to a knighthood and
became Sir John Pudding. The ironic reference is to the gains
made by the Barons after King John signed Magna Carta and
the writer expresses dismay that such a momentous occasion is
now ridiculed, 'for now every Fool at a Fair, or Zany at a
Mountebank's Stage, is call'd Jack Pudding, has a Gridiron at
his back, and a great Pair of Spectacles at his Buttocks, to
ridicule the most noble Order of the Gridiron' (p. 61). Gordon
or Arbuthnot write as devil's advocate, defending all present-
day 'Barons', for nothing, not even the world itself, can escape
physical associations with Pudding and the article concludes
rhetorically:

Why should we then be Laughed out of Pudding and Dumpling? or why
ridiculed out of Good Living? Plots and Politicks may hurt us, but Pudding
cannot. Let us therefore adhere to Pudding, and keep ourselves out of
Harm's way; according to the Golden Rule laid down by a celebrated
Dumpling Eater now defunct;
>   Be of your Patron's Mind, what e'er he says:
>   Sleep very much; Think little, and Talk less:
>   Mind neither Good nor Bad, nor Right nor Wrong;
>   But Eat your *Pudding*, Fool, and hold your Tongue
>   MATHEW PRIOR

Prior is said to show wisdom by making the title of these lines
'Merry Andrew' and not 'Jack Pudding', 'which Name my
friend *Matt.* could not hear with Temper, as carrying with it an
oblique Reflection on Sir *John Pudding,* the Hero of this
DUMPLEID'. And if any person reverts to calling Fools, Jack
Pudding, no punishment would be too great for them. Prior's
poem was written in 1718 and according to *The Gentleman's
Magazine* of 1777 it originated in an ironic observation when
Prior was travelling with the Bishop of Winchester. They saw a
mountebank act in which the Fool stuffed his mouth with
pudding while holding a stag's tongue in the other, and his
master remarked 'Hold your tongue and eat your pudding'.
The ironic observation on the times probably derived from the
act, and the Bishop was said to have remarked, 'This fellow is no
fool'. Two years after *The Dumpleid,* the first actor of Macheath
in Gay's *The Beggars' Opera,* Tom Walker, was satirized by John
Leigh as a Pudding for offering the following services to a
gullible patron of the arts in hopes of a reward. 'I'll be as
diverting as ever I can,/I will by the faith of a sinner!/I mimic all
actors, the worst and the best,/I'll sing him a song, I'll crack
him a jest . . . I beg he'd invite me to dinner' (Chetwood, p.
180). And in June 1735, *The Craftsman* published a long article
'In defence of Strollers'. The strollers in this case were the new
breed of ambassadors, travelling throughout Europe. The
figure under polite attack was one J. Marral, and Marral was a
common name in the country for a Lord of Misrule (see
Chapter 7). However, this man is shown to have his own kind of
versatility. 'It is impossible to tell in how many Shapes He hath
appeared, for the Service of his Country. He hath been a

Jack-Pudding, a *Ballad-Singer* . . . He can likewise play the *Droll*
to Admiration [and is] one of the *greatest political Strollers* any Age
or Nation ever produced'.[9] No mountebanking is included and
so we assume that Mr Marral's intentions were honest if not
always the most dignified. The same journal had also carried an
indignant report, which I think was not satirical, on one of the
most popular diversions in Bartholomew Fair in 1727. Its lack
of patriotism horrified the writer. 'There were *two Jack-puddings*
entertaining the Popellace from a gallery on the Outside of one
of the *Booths*; one of whom represented an *Englishman* and the
other a *Spaniard,* and the Spaniard knocked down the Englishman' (Rosenfeld, p. 122). Such an affront to decency was
further accentuated by the fact that the 'Parcel of *infamous
Strollers*' were not brought before the law and made an example
of, but instead were allowed to undermine the morals of the
people with impunity. It is clear that morality and dignity had
become synonymus as the following chapter shows, and that
John Bull, who had originally been a caricature was becoming a
national hero.

However, political satire continued. In 1738 the struggle
between Whigs and Tories was carried in *The Gentleman's
Magazine* as a story of upstart Dumplings rebelling against their
old and distinguished masters, the family of Puddings, whereas
everyone knew that *Jack Pudding* had more wit than *Diddle
Dumpling* as well as greater antiquity. Plots were revealed which
were intended to cause dissension among the Pudding family.
The Plain Puddings of the country were being made jealous of
the City Plumb Puddings, and the Black Puddings (from the
North) were being won over to the Dumpling side. Finally,
foreign alignment had been brought in. The Dumplings were
negotiating with the French Jean Potages. 'Eat your Pudding
and hold your tongue' was clearly an expression of the intention
to usurp the Pudding's inheritance. A defence of the Dumplings
appeared later in the year, when a correspondent refuted any
allegations that the family of Dumpling would 'descend to eat
dirty Puddings'.[10] At the same time that playwrights used
Harlequin and his companions in the battle for standards in
plays and mountebank entertainers flourished in the country,
Pudding-fool satire continued. *The London Gazetteer* adopted as

editiorial name the Fool, to which satirical letters could be addressed. One of the wittiest is that written on 29 December 1748, immediately after the treaty of Aix-la-Chapelle, brought about by the French to establish peace in Europe. 'To the Fool . . . I Have a Brother Fool who told me a Foolish Joke lately' about the 'feating and regaling' of all the countries of Europe at Aix-la-Chapelle; eating a new pudding concocted by the French. 'The Germans took some to Vienna but it suited not the Austrian stomach.' The brother Fool had been sick on tasting it but the writer fears 'as French Dishes are much in Fashion, and Curiosity may tempt our English Palates to try and eat of this new Dish, it may endanger an Epidemical Sickness among them'.

After the mid-eighteenth century the Pudding terminology declined, as did satire itself, although the popularity of mountebanks and their Jack Puddings continued. A second edition of the 1700 *Harangues* of mountebanks was printed in 1762, with a prefatory warning against sedentary, back-street quacks. However, at the end, the performing doctor receives one of his last analogies with the politician.

> The politician . . . finding how the people are taken with specious miraculous impossibilities, plays the game . . . So you see the politician is, and must be, a mountebank in state affairs; and the mountebank . . . if he thrives, is an errant politician. [p. 21]

Attitudes throughout society differed from the literary fashion. Whereas mountebanks were still so popular that there was at least one fatality due to the crowds which went to see them,[11] journals became more serious. *The Methodist* in 1766 still made a rather weak appeal to its followers through pudding analogy,[12] but increasingly this became the exception. J.T. Smith in 1815 recalled with nostalgia the days when Jack Pudding appeared at Bartholomew Fair, and other writers of the nineteenth century showed a similar leaning to the past without seeming to have been aware of their contemporary Fools, who continued quite strongly outside London. The reasons for this change in attitude are the subject of the next chapters. The Fool still had his role in society, as illustrations of capped and belled figures on ropes show.[13] However, by the end of the eighteenth century it became possible to divide the progress of the Fool into three separate roads; one led to the increasing number of respectable comedians, another grew from Grimaldi's unique transformation of the bumpkin-clown into Harlequin's successor and third was the continuation of folk-Fool practices in rural parts of England and even in London.

CHAPTER 6

The Respectability of the Fool and the rise of the clown

Social behaviour became increasingly influenced by the dignity of man in worldly terms rather than cosmic laws. By the end of the eighteenth century respectability was the key code of behaviour and, not surprisingly, this influenced the attitudes to the Fool and even his own view of himself. As already stated, *The Gentleman's Magazine* doesn't mention Jack Pudding after 1750. New satirical journals, such as *The Devil* and *The Devil's Pocket-Book* (1786) emulated the higher tone and called their political attacks 'serio-comic'. Not even *The Comic Magazine* of 1796 makes any reference to fairs, mountebanks or their companions. The humour is genteel and would lead one to think that entertainments such as fairs had succumbed to the numerous decrees against them, were it not for the information gathered by Sybil Rosenfeld and publications such as an anonymous childrens' journal which appeared in Shropshire in 1820. This begins with 'come Tom, make haste, the Fair is begun. Here is Jack Pudding with the gridiron on his back, and all the boys hallooing'.[1] The picture of boys chasing or following the Fool curiously resembles the image raised by Kirchmaier in the sixteenth century and supports the conclusion that the fundamental basis of local entertainments remained the same until the nineteenth century, particularly in rural areas. Writers and other respectable people looked down on fairgrounds as topics for adults, and saw them as toys for children. It's fortunate, therefore, that the Shropshire magazine contains a lively example of dialogue between the 'doctor' and his Andrew. The Fool constantly undermines the claims of his master—and so shows that travelling 'doctors' were there to entertain rather than deceive. The Fool puts an end to the offer of cures with the song, 'he who is healthy, and cheerful and cool/Yet squanders his money on physic's a *fool.*/Fool, master, fool, fool.' So the doctor then changes his tactics and tempts the audience to buy with the promise that in one packet someone will find a gold ring. At which the Fool advises his master to buy them all himself, since he could do with that kind of money. The whole dialogue is comic repartee such as is found among comedians today, but was not found any more in adult journals of the period. *The Devil* likens one politician, who may be William Pitt, to a quack doctor but gives no details. Morley's *History of Bartholomew Fair* shows that the centre of fairground inspiration didn't decay until 1830, when 'the nation had outgrown it', and the London fair was last proclaimed in 1855. As one pun in *The Comic Magazine* of 1832 put it: 'the *fair* of every *stage* was exceedingly *reduc'd*'. The entertainments which grew up were mechanical. Punch, who had begun his entertaining life as a man became the puppet we know today. Even the unconventional magazine, *The Merry-go-Round*, printed in London in 1894, proclaims 'the Fun of the Fair' and the booths and the shows but calls 'bah! to the humbug and tricks/Of the quacks who are more than "renowned" '. Since "renown'd" was the old claim made two centuries earlier, we know that some mountebanks persevered into the late nineteenth century although the metropolitan attitude towards them was changed.

As might be expected in an age of growing respectability, comedians such as Edward Shuter and Charles Dibdin, who began their careers after 1720, and were booth manager/professional comedian and writer/solo comedian respectively, grew up with a sense of value of their own dignity. As already mentioned, Shuter was reputed to have earned more in Bartholomew Fair than in the licensed theatres and it's also rumoured that in the mid-eighteenth century he took the initiative in discomforting Garrick when that celebrity went to Bartholomew Fair. It is said that Shuter refused to take money from him saying that fairground people do not take from each other. The height of Shuter's success was from about 1755 to 1762 and the form his entertainment took in the Fair was a variety of Drolls and he specialized in comic advertisements for them, satirizing the grandiloquent claims usually made. In 1759 he announced that 'On the Grand Parade, immediately

after the Fair is proclaimed the bold Shuter will review his
Troop; and the Public are earnestly requested critically and
optically to observe, that the full Figure, which will appear in
the Middle of the Platform, is the Chief of the Cherokeese,
Shawanese, Tyconderageese, Catabawa and Catawawa or
Sachem of the Five Nations' (Rosenfeld, p. 61). Despite this,
Shuter was always in control and conscious of his own respectability. The closest he came to Joe Haines' character was in
1761, and this was through the content of his advertisement
rather than his own behaviour. The announcement for that
year was that the plays contained the 'essence of Comicality,
prepared by the Directions of Dr Shuter . . . For the certain
Cure of the Spleen' (p. 62). He never acted the Fool, like
Haines, but presented prepared comedy. For example, when he
found his comic reputation acting to his social disadvantage he
disengaged himself with wit and composure.

> This child of humour was at dinner one day, in a promiscuous company
> and, as soon as the cloth was taken away, one of them got up and entreated
> . . . he would be comical. 'God', said Shuter, 'I forgot my fool's dress—but,
> however I'll go and fetch it, if you'll be my substitute till I return'. The
> man thought this very comical, and declared he would.[2]

Of course Shuter never returned and so reversed the joke
onto the perpetrator.

Another careful comedian was Charles Dibdin (1745-1814)
and today his greatest claim to fame is that his natural son,
Charles, was to be one of the moving spirits behind the success
of Joe Grimaldi. Charles senior was a solo entertainer, singer
and raconteur and in his travels round the country he too met
with expectations that he would act the Fool at dinner. In
Colchester in 1787 he met with 'an unfortunate and truly
ridiculous circumstance' at a dinner with eight gentlemen of the
town. The invitation to supper 'meant nothing more than that I
should relieve the *pipe* and *tabor,* by doing my utmost *to entertain
the company'* and Dibdin goes on to explain that 'when I am stuck
up in my temporary orchestra and playing my tricks I am
unconditionally at the devotion of the audience. Before or after
. . . I cannot consent to consider myself in an ineligible light'.[3] It
may well be that some rural communities still had a rougher

sense of humour than Londoners for in the most extraordinary
revelations Thomas Turner of East Hoathly tells us personal
details such as: 'Wed. 22nd January, 1757. After supper our
behaviour was far from that of serious, harmless mirth; it was
down right obstreperious, mixed with a great deal of folly and
stupidity. Our diversion was dancing or jumping about without
any violin'. His diary makes constant reference to 'drunk again'
and 'sure I am a direct fool'. And the most curious 'revel' took
place in Turner's house. It began at 6 a.m. when Turner's
companions surprised him in his bed, dragged him out naked
and dressed him partly in man's and partly in woman's
clothes—his wife's petticoats—'and in this manner they made
me dance without shoes and stockings until they had emptied
the bottle of wine, and also a bottle of my beer'.[4] Few diarists
make such frank confessions; Turner's gives a picture of rural
life in the eighteenth century which reveals a gap in official
proprieties and the real behaviour of men after they were well
and truly inebriated. It may have been this divergence of
expectations which led to conflict when entertainers were
invited to dine. Dibdin's hosts finally thought his sobriety 'the
dirty impudence of a depredating itinerant'. But there were
times when Dibdin's request for respect received unexpected
support. In Newark in 1789 he 'ate a dinner, remarkably well
dressed' and ordered French dishes. The inn-keeper treated
him as 'UN MY LOR' until he was told the man was only an
actor and then he virtually threw him out. On Dibdin's return
to Newark he happened to be taken by Lord and Lady Lincoln
to dine at the same inn. It isn't often that hypocrisy is exposed
so neatly, and much can be excused if travelling, solo comedians
preferred to keep their public strictly behind the footlights. It is
interesting to find, however, that Dibdin enjoyed playing in the
ancient Fool home of Beverley where, he said, the inhabitants
appeared both independent and mixed without snobbery.
However, in other parts of the country, the importance of
establishing a touring company's propriety shows in many
advertisements of the time. As early as 1735 a Norwich
company playing in London called themselves 'artificial
comedians', to allay any doubts as to their professionalism and
social respectability. They were clearly unaware of the

sixteenth-century implications of being 'artificial'. And the
epitome for a claim to comic dignity comes from the epitaph for
Mr Benjamin Griffin of Drury-Lane theatre:

> Reader, this Humble Stone demands your Praise, For beneath
>   an Actor lies; . . .
> Cou'd the most rigid with chaste Mirth beguile,
> And from just Reason force an honest smile; . . .
> For greater Worth in Private was he lov'd;
> Mirth without Folly, Friendship without Art.
>   [*Gentleman's Magazine, March 1740, p. 132*]

There were low-comedians whose working life began earlier
and who retained a taste for the eccentric; for example
Pinkethman and Bullock, two more actors at the turn of the
eighteenth century who were not ashamed to profit from
Bartholomew Fair among a variety of fairground and folk performers:

> A comic Droll here ev'ry Hour is shewn;
> Here *Robin Hood* and *Little John* are known:
> A City Rake, a noble King appears;
> His Tinsel Dress each gazing Clown [audience] reveres.
>   [Rosenfeld, p. 22.]

One other man born the previous century was Joe Trefusis and
he was a well-loved, professional clown on stage and off.
Although he was the original Trapland in Congreve's *Love for
Love*, he was especially known for dancing the 'awkward
Country Clown' and in this role he appeared at court in 1698.
Trefusis was reputed to be the illegitimate son of Oliver
Cromwell, born in Ireland in the mid-seventeenth century.
However W.R. Chetwood treats this as myth. There was no
physical resemblance. '*Jo* had a long Chin, and naturally a most
consummate foolish Face by Nature formed for suitable characters; yet a person of infinite Humour, and shrewd Conceits'. He
was one clown who retained some public favour for the clown
and began the long road back from considering the country
cully as the nadir of society. Chetwood gives an example of the
style of Joe's performance. General Ingoldby admired his talent
to the extent of sending five guineas to the stage door. The next

day Joe dressed smartly and went to thank the General, but was not recognized until he changed his behaviour: *'Ise th' very Man, an't please your Ex-cell-en-cey*; and at the same time, twirling his Hat, as he did in the Dance with his consummate foolish Face and Scrape'. At this the General gave him another five guineas and Joe made his exit in the same awkward, clownish manner which 'set the table on a roar'. Another example of his sense of humour comes in an anecdote of his fishing by the Liffey, dressed in full fishing gear. A boat of theatre acquaintances came by from Dublin on its way to London. Trefusis offered to see them down the river but omitted to get off until they reached London. Eventually, Robert Wilks found him, still in his fishing outfit, gazing at the clock in Covent Garden. When asked what he was doing 'in that pickle', Joe replied, ' "Hum! Ha! why faith, Bobby . . . I only came from Dublin to see what it was o'Clock at Covent Garden" ' (Chetwood pp. 169-70). Another eccentric who combined intelligence with fooling and was possibly the last maintained household jester in England was known as Lord Flame. His real name, Samuel Johnson, would not have given the right impression of his means of living bearing in mind the larger figure of the period of that name and Johnson rarely used his proper name. To begin with he was a dancing master, author and musician. In the 1720s he was engaged by the Duke of Montague to add fuel to the fire of theatrical battles by writing the play, *Hurlothrumbo*, which 'for absurd bombast and turgid nonsense perhaps stands unrivalled in the English language'. The Duke extolled the play in the papers as the most sublime effort of human genius 'and in consequence [it] was performed for 30 successive nights . . . until the whole town found itself duped'[5] Evidence of clear wit by Johnson appears in a letter in *The Gentleman's Magazine* for March 1758. The only evidence we have that this is by him is that it is signed 'Hurlothrumbo', and were someone else to have borrowed the name, there would undoubtedly have been a ripost by Johnson later. The letter is headed 'To a Methodist Preacher', for like the Quakers in the previous century, the new sect of Methodist preaching came in for a period of scepticism towards it. Under the heading Johnson wrote *si populus vult decipi, decipiatur* (if the people wish to be deceived, let them be deceived). Johnson wrote as a mountebank who sees the preacher's activities as complementary to his own and expresses this in an obvious parody of the well-known Pauline Epistle:

> Are the mob your customers, so are they mine? are you the scorn and jest of men of sense, so am I? In a word, if you turn the brain of your patients, it may be affirmed, with equal truth, that I often destroy the constitution of mine.

Collaboration is offered on the following terms: 'when I find my patients departing I will turn them over to your care; converts are easily made in a dying hour, and a *will* may be drawn in your favour as *methodical* as you please. On the other hand [when your patients degenerate into real madness] send 'em to me. From your affectionate brother, HURLOTHRUMBO'.

As London became the more genteel and stable in theatrical ventures, the satirist, in his later years retired to Gawsworth Hall in Cheshire, where he stayed until his death in 1773. He kept his title of Lord Flame, and always behaved as if he were of the rank of Lord, and his 'lively sallies of wit' made him permanently acceptable both at Gawsworth and in houses of neighbouring gentlemen. Johnson needed financial assistance and this was brought to him annually, under the pretence of repayment of debts and of income. His eccentricities were accepted even by the local people. Behind his back they may have called him 'Old Maggoty' but:

> the rustics celebrate him as a remarkably excellent performer on the violin . . . They add too, that he . . . imagined he was an uncommonly melodious singer, but the contortions of his face during the performance, were so hideous, that he was accustomed to stand with his face close to a wall, and to cover each side of it with his hands . . . as otherwise it would have been sure to have diverted all attention from his song.[6]

Finally, his unconventionality continued after his death. He was buried, as requested, in a small wood near the village and in the grounds of Gawsworth Hall. The reason for this consistently irreverent choice of resting place is given on the burial stone. His own epitaph declares that 'When he rose again, laid here alone,/No friend and he should quarrel for a Bone'. Even worse, 'were some lame old Gossip nigh/She possibly might take his leg or thigh'. A later stone was placed nearby, with solemn sentiments which not only counteract the humour of the first but give the impression that the jester had gone to a place from which resurrection was unlikely:

> If chance hath brought thee here, or curious eyes,
> To see a spot where this poor jester lies,
> A thoughtless jester even in his death,
> Uttering jibes beyond his latest breath . . .
> Look on that stone and this and ponder well:
> Then choose 'twixt Life and Death, 'twixt
> Heaven and Hell.   [Earwater, p. 571]

The heavy morality, which had nothing to do with a knowledge of earlier theology, only has the effect of making Johnson's lightheartedness more appreciable. His initiation into the theatre in the 1720s, before respectability became so important, may well have contributed to his carefree attitude towards his profession and towards graver matters. Like Trefusis he saw no harm in acting the 'Pudding' at table and his jesting abilities brought their own kind of respect. Later comedians applied a stricter professionalism. An interesting intermediary was William Parsons. He made no personal contribution to the dignity debate, yet his highly popular performances at Covent Garden, Drury Lane and Lincoln's Inn Fields, drew aesthetic arguments for and against him. Between 1762 and 1795 there was hardly a year when he did not feature in the London theatre (though not at Bartholomew Fair) and his last appearance was as 'Dupe' in Drury Lane's Christmas show. Thomas Bellamy's 1795 biography of Parsons clarifies the expectations of high society as regards the low-comedian and draws distinctions between the comedian's talents and the crudity of the buffoon or Fool. Bellamy refutes those who said buffoonery and grimace were Parson's only talents. Such comments vilified the actor's artistic abilities and Bellamy called it the CANT OF CRITICISM. However his conclusions place Parsons in the 'fool' camp, howsoever gifted, for Bellamy defends Parsons by saying the actor possessed a combination of gifts; English humour, Italian gesticulation and French locomotion, whereby he could 'ingeniously convulse both audience and actors'. Further 'his unforced stratagems' were those expected in the Farces in which he appeared. Finally, it was Parson's good-humour within his inventiveness which made his antics irresistibly comic. So in Parsons we have a further development in the revival of the hybrid clown, who finally came into his own through Joseph Grimaldi.

This is not to deny that the eighteenth century was Harlequin's heyday in English theatre. Willson Disher goes so far as to point out that after Harlequin's introduction no other character has ever made so many appearances on the English stage. Much of Harlequin's success was due to John Rich who, under the name Lun, devised Harlequin entertainments between 1717 and 1761. By 1740 the clown had become Harlequin's servant, instead of the reverse. As Andrew Halliday wrote, 'in Mr. Rich's pantomimes the harlequin was the principal character, the hero in fact [and] the clown was a very inferior part, less in importance than even pantaloon and pierrot'. However, opinions have differed. Disher later observed that though the Italian *Commedia Dell'Arte* troups came to England at their most 'formidable peak' when the English Fool 'was discarded according to the accident of a lost tradition [yet] English Harlequinades . . . were but dim shadows of the scintillating inventions of the Italian originals'.[7] The word 'hero' gives clues to the change. Harlequin in England was famous for his dexterity not, as Addison noted when he visited Italy, for gross blunders. Much of this was probably due to John Rich's personal talent. When Harlequin was first adopted by writers such as Aphra Behn, Howard and Mountfort, he was a speaking character, and in the farcical version of *Dr Faustus* it is his blundering into Scaramouche's den, and the blunders he survives, which contribute to the comedy. Yet, it is from Lun's success that the myth of Harlequin being first performed in dumb-show in England has derived. John Rich was greatly gifted in visual dexterity and bizarre mime, but vocally he was weak and had what would have been thought a crude accent. Halliday notes that it was Rich who 'closed Harlequin's mouth' and with physical versatility alone kept him in the limelight and the clown in the shade. What is surprising is that Rich's invention lasted for so long. It has been thought by some that David Garrick successfully reintroduced a speaking Harlequin in *Harlequin's Invasion,* first performed in 1759. However, it is interesting to note that *The London Stage* (ed. A.L. Avery) records the following comment about that first production. 'The author expected a speaking Harlequin, Pantaloon, Pierrot, Mezzetin, &c. but found the customary figures banished for the substitution of a "stupid Taylor and his more stupid wife" (vol. 2, p. 766). It seems not to have been until after Rich's death in 1761 that the speaking Harlequin became acceptable to audiences. Also, by some strange coincidence, William Parson's career as English clown also began to rise during 1762. Garrick's 1763 production of *Harlequin's Invasion* achieved a Harlequin who dared once more to speak, but in the Prologue Garrick apologizes for this and at the same time pays tribute to Rich:

> But why a speaking Harlequin? 'Tis wrong,
> Tho wits will say, to give the fool a tongue. [reference to
>   Mathew Prior's satiric poem]
> When Lun appeared, with matchless art and whim
> He gave the power of speech to every limb;
> Tho' masked and mute, conveyed his quick intent,
> And told in frolic gestures all he meant;
> But now the motley coat, and sword of wood,
> Require a tongue to make them understood.   [Prologue]

And the clown began his fresh popularity through Parson, Grimaldi-père and Jean-Baptiste Dubois.

The change involved the gradual change in dress to the spectacular, visual effect of the clown, which in essence has lasted to the present day. Halliday argued that the Harlequin was initially and accidentally reduced to being 'a mere dancer and posturer' by the change of his costume from the loose jacket and trousers, in which he had freedom of movement, to a close fitting white silk garment covered in spangles. This dress is remarkably close to the one we associate with Grimaldi and I think we may see the innovation as one stage in a general change. Charles Dibdin Junior, is very specific about dress and says that all clowns before Grimaldi Junior wore outré dress

and red faces like their country ancestors. The illustration in
Pasquin (1740) shows that for quite some time parti-colouring
was also a possibility. The later biography of Dubois (1762-
1818) supports Dibdin. It would seem that rustic appearance
contrasted better with Harlequin's form of parti-colouring than
the old English Fool's dress on the clown. Dubois began his
career in England with the famous equestrian show of Astley,
who opened his new venture in 1770 and Dubois joined about
1780. Astley's Amphitheatre combined trick shows, horsemanship and clowns and is the famous birthplace of the circus.
Dubois became 'clown to the horsemanship' and Findlater
gives an account of all the talents of Dubois who despite his
French origins was accomplished in many English fairground
and folk tricks. Many of course were common to several
countries. Dubois excelled as acrobat, juggler and tumbler and
was known

> for an act in which he spun thirteen funnel-shaped caps, hooked them up
> one by one with his feet, and then caught them all on his head; while
> another of his special feats—sometimes performed between the acts of
> more solemn fare at Drury Lane—was to dance the traditional 'egg
> hornpipe' in wooden clogs.   [Findlater, p. 55]

The funnel-shaped caps are those known today as fools' caps
and in the nineteenth century they were used by some
mumming troups. The egg hornpipe meant dancing blindfold
in clogs backwards and forwards through a dozen or so
positioned eggs.

In Dibdin's eyes Dubois was the best clown after old
Grimaldi's exit and until the young Grimaldi established
himself. Then Dubois parted from the Dibdin management and
continued successfully at Covent Garden. Findlater
emphasizes the innovatory spirit of Dubois, which probably
had an influence on the young Grimaldi. Contemporary claims
at this period of change in theatre, circus and pantomime are
conflicting and Dibdin himself is not slow to claim originality.
However, his account coincides with the date that Dubois left
his theatre and is not entirely egotistical; therefore, some
credence may be valid. We already have Halliday's report that
Harlequin contributed to his own demise by changing to a

white dress. Findlater comes to the conclusion that the Italian clown, Pierrot, was the most important factor. However, Dibdin claims that it was himself who gave the helping hand in 1800. In the pantomime, *Peter Wilkins,* in which Dubois and Grimaldi appeared together for the last time, Dibdin designed two new costumes for the clowns 'more extravagant than it had been the custom for such characters to wear, and from that time—at the Wells at least—the Costume of the Clown was completely changed; and a whimsical mixture of colours and compositions invariably studied'. The make-up was Grimaldi's. Dubois (and it is implied Joe's father) 'never dressed himself otherwise than as a rustic booby, with red hair, and painted his face merely in imitation of florid nature . . . The present mode of dressing Clowns and painting their faces, was then invented by Mr. G. who, in every respect, founded a *New School* for Clowns'.[8] Findlater is wise in drawing careful conclusions. For example, the make-up gradually became more and more exaggerated. Halliday stresses that compared with the clown's dress of 1863, Grimaldi's changes were moderate and he did not obliterate his personal facial expression with the white chalk and paint. The first illustration of Grimaldi (Findlater, p. 141) confirms this. But the talent of Grimaldi was too much for Dubois to compete with and he continued to shine 'with undiminished rays' in more traditional fooling at Covent Garden. However, George Cruikshank's famous illustration of Grimaldi-père hurling young Joey into the pit is not strictly accurate, since the father is given white clown's make-up at its most extreme and an elaborate costume to match. The illustration is dated 1836.

The importance of Grimaldi in the history of the professional Fool cannot be overvalued. As Cruikshank's drawing shows, rustic dress and parti-colouring were abandoned in favour of white, and advertisements show that the fairground Fool tended to follow the same example. Charles Dickens accidentally shows this in his Preface to *The memoirs of Joseph Grimaldi* (1838):

We have lost that clown now;—he is still alive, though, for we saw him only the day before last Bartholomew Fair, eating a real saveloy, and we are

> sorry to say he had deserted to the illegitimate drama, for he was seated on one of 'Clark's Circus' waggons:- we have lost that Clown [Grimaldi] and that pantomime.   [p. vii.]

Dicken's repeated reference to 'that clown' who was lost, when so many copies had been propagated is explained by David Mayer. Harlequin had dominated the pantomime by his tricks and dramatic surprises; he had never in any way been satiric himself. However, the new Fool stimulated new pantomimic effects which 'progressed from a cheerful and somewhat mindless entertainment to the only effective means of satire to hold the stage in the first thirty years of the nineteenth century [for Grimaldi, Dibdin and later Farley] diverted the harlequinade of Rich, dominated by Harlequin and consequently emphasizing knockabout pursuit and gymnastic feats, to a harlequinade dominated by Clown and consequently emphasizing comedy and satire' (p. 6). Mayer points out that the licensing authorities tried to impose those restrictions which had helped discourage fairground Fools in their satire. Nevertheless, the range of comic subjects pursued by the clown during the first thirty years of his revival were as wide as Jack Pudding's and extended to the Crown and the poor; to questions of religious tolerance, and the conduct of the Napoleonic war and much of the satire was of a high standard. After the retirement of Grimaldi in 1828 pantomime lost this satiric edge, developing instead scenic extravaganza so that by the end of the century the pantomime clown was frequently a stereotyped figure, whose role was indistinguishable from that of other characters.

PETER PATERSON—CLOWN-MANQUÉ

Stories of clowns in the nineteenth century are rife and I have chosen the autobiography of James Glass Bertram, alias Peter Paterson, *Glimpses of Real Life*, written after the young man had made a vigorous, humorous and varied trial of the theatre. His story is valuable because it covers such a wide range of travelling theatrical ventures and shows how a failed, serious actor could become booth player, stroller and circus clown. And the editor of the 1864 edition brings many of these strands together when he recalls the heyday of strolling players:

> We can remember the days when the old strolling player was an institution
> of the country—as, indeed, in some remote parts he still is—and when the
> annual visit of the strolling company would awaken the curiosity of 'the
> town'. Then, the wonderfully smart-looking gentleman, dressed in the
> sharply defined hat, the tight-fitting but very threadbare coat   [Preface]

came first through the town with his family. Paterson discloses
further that the rest of the company arrived by night to conceal
their poorer dress. However, the editor is full of nostalgia for the
troup and writes of the pre-performance procession through the
town, led by the low-comedian (who doubled, when necessary
as clown). His outdoor dress is reminiscent of the mountebank
or mumming doctor, or even of Chaplin, rather than a painted
clown. As he led the procession, the town saw 'a grave-looking
individual, but with a twinkle in his eye—always carrying an
umbrella, with its point in front of himself, as if to keep off those
mobs of urchins whom he had on sundry occasions made to roar
with delight at what he called his "mugs", and who would insist
upon congregating round him' (p. 5). Paterson's own career
began with an over-ambitious debut as Hamlet in a Scottish
provincial theatre. The confidence which he eloquently expresses took hold of him in the wings, evaporated into total
silence on facing the audience. He pulled faces to try to make
the struggle that of the character not the actor, but the welcom-
ing applause of the audience soon turned to hisses and boos.
Paterson recalls looking down at his threadbare black costume
and thinking 'what would my mother say if she saw me making
such an infernal fool of myself'. An appreciative roar of laughter
revealed to him that he had thought aloud. He conveniently
passed out and so exited the tragedian and entered the
comedian. Soon after this he was playing the clown in *Twa
Drovers*. Ambition took him south of the border and it was here
he found employment with an established theatre difficult, so
he was forced to join a Booth company in Birkenhead.
However, one point of note is that the shares system which the
first Elizabethan companies worked by was still carried on in
Booth theatre management. But with that any comparison
ends, for the manner of playing was very rough. To attract an

audience, the low comedian, usually dressed as a clown, came outside to make as much fun as he could, 'mugging' (ie. pulling faces) while the rest of the company danced to far from perfect music. Full-length plays were absurdly cut to make a half-hour's entertainment and the manager stood at the side of the stage giving directions to actors as to when to go on and which parts of the play to cut. As can be expected there were frequent backstage disputes during the performance.

Paterson's sudden change to circus clown came through his nostalgia for legitimate theatre. He met, by chance, a Dickensian character called Mr Chirper in a Birmingham Inn and was then and there invited to join Chirper's Circus as clown. Paterson thought that time would have to be spent first for him to learn the art of clowning; and Mr Chirper's reply illustrates the bizarre degree to which the art had deteriorated: 'Rely upon it, turning clown is the easiest thing in the world . . . as for the jokes, never fear man. The Ringmaster has all the old standard ones ready cut and dry; and as for a new supply . . . you can soon get up a few by reading *Punch* or *The Family Herald*'. The technique was the exact opposite of Hamlet's advice to clowns and ironically, since Paterson had begun with serious Shakespearean ambitions, the fashionable jokes were parodies of Shakespeare combined with 'mugging'. Paterson's first inspired suggestion was that he might pull a face for a while and then say 'to draw or not to draw, that is the question'. What is even more curious, such crude parodies were taken as serious renditions by continental historians, who were much taken by the English clown. In 1890 Le Roux and Garnier wrote *Acrobats and Mountebanks* and said of the English clown that at home 'the *jester* . . . appears in white tights, ornamented with blue or red patches indiscriminately arranged, with a short drapery round the hips, and a fool's cap on his head. Thus attired he does not caper and joke, but declaims passages from Shakespeare and sings Irish songs which delight the public in the cheap places' (p. 278). The Shakespearean passages were of course part of capering and joking. There were 'gagging' clowns, of which Paterson was one and there were acrobatic clowns. Paterson said of both that 'a good clown knows how to keep the ball rolling and the crowd in a good humour [for] an immense deal of

fun may be made out of nothing'. However there's nothing to
suggest that the gagging clown used contemporary subjects as
satire. The examples given show how he had returned to the
somewhat mindless entertainment of Harlequin. Even on tour
no comments were made: spectacle was what the audience
looked for and circuses, such as Mr Chirper's, were growing in
size and popularity replacing 'the little mountebank parties
that used to pay an annual visit to the village green, and delight
the rustic sightseers . . . by giving away an occasional fat pig'
(Paterson, p. 122).

The mountebank parties mentioned here would seem to
mean successful groups of strollers. 'Mountebanking' in circus
slang usually meant tricking the audience, and the most
extreme example is that of an animal showman whose stock had
died save for one bear. He shaved the poor creature and dressing it in woman's clothes he tied it to a chair to present it as 'the
pig-faced lady'. By this means he earned enough money to
replenish his proper show. Common mountebanking was the
painting of horses so that all appeared the smooth cream colour
of a pedigree. Paterson doesn't accuse Chirper's of such decep-
tion and he gives a detailed picture of both the part the circus
played in the touring programme and the reactions of the
people, who came first to the hiring fair for business, pouring in
from all parts of the surrounding country. After the buying and
selling the band would play: 'and the crowds on the street
divide to each side. "it's the show-folk! It's the show-folk!" is
now the cry, and onward we sweep in grand procession, headed
by a band, the musicians sitting in an elegant carriage
. . .drawn by six splendid cream-coloured horses. The company
followed in pairs, dressed like cavaliers and ladies of the olden
time. Reader, your humble servant brought up the rear of the
procession, dressed as a clown, riding on a gaily caparisoned
donkey! . . . bursts of laughter waited upon the clown. The fool
was the great feature of this scene, and there he sat, grave as a
judge, with his face tailward, unmoved by the cries of 'Oh, but
look at the fool!" "Look at the fool!" "Here be the show-folk",
&c. In country places "the show folk" is the universal name
given [to] all visiting performers' (p. 169). Paterson's un-
dignified posture was originally a folk game of mockery for

henpecked or deceived husbands. It was Joseph Haines who brought this custom into his act as he moved from town to town. After his death a rhyme went, 'Joe Haines is dead and left his *Ass* behind! . . . Must Haines depart while asses multiply'.[9] Despite the fact that Paterson was not required to do difficult acrobatics he found the strain of the life telling on him and went once more in search of a strolling company. He tried 'tavern-theatre'—the forerunner of music-hall, but was obliged to spend most of his wages on drink. He found that family companies of strollers which the editor remembered were nearly all broken up because the railways now allowed movement from the country to the town. Paterson reached his nadir in London and gave up the struggle, to return home and write the above book, which we are grateful for for its panoramic coverage of life outside the London theatres.

No matter what the comedian's means of entertainment were, the expression 'fool' became an increasingly pejorative one (except in rural communities); low-comedian, clown and even jester were preferred. Lear's Fool was respected in productions of Shakespeare's play and Fool's dress was used for other classical 'clowns' and also in Christmas home entertainments. Otherwise clown had become the respected term after a start of being the country cully, totally devoid of respect. Also, as he lost his satiric individuality in England, he became the continental star performer. According to Le Roux and Garnier, it was the English clown which started the universal trend in circuses. They wrote in 1890 that Pierrot and Italian pantomime had become an extinct art. 'They are now effaced, dispelled by the cloud of powder which the clown, launched from the other side of the Channel, scattered in the air as he tumbled upon the French stage' (p. 278). If they are not exaggerating, then it was the English clown who instigated the circus clown's international fame in figures such as Grock; ironically at a time when the clown's role in England had become a series of predictable tricks. However, he still had a professional role to play, whereas the parti-coloured Fool was reserved for private entertainment, and folk Fools had their own tradition, which had been influenced by fairground characters. Several mumming characters reflect itinerants. Poverty-stricken strollers, who were dressed nearly in tatters and vitually had to beg for payment were known as mummers by the mid-nineteenth century and one particularly moving example was the solo performer, the penny showman, who 'fights his battle of life, industriously wandering from one fair to another, in many instances with the show on his back, and accompanied perhaps by his better half, carrying a child' (Paterson, p. 123). In the eyes of town society, the clown was at his best as a Christmas pantomime entertainer, while the Fool only continued to exist in rural folk traditions.

CHAPTER 7

Seasonal Fooling

In returning to folk play the circle is completed. The source from which Fools and clowns had risen to professional status reappears in nineteenth-century texts and with the Fool still centre of attraction. Many theories have been put forward and certain observations, though necessary, are obvious. For example, interpolations in mumming texts of the comic pieces from known plays, such as *Mucidorus*, couldn't have occurred before those plays were written. Similarly, the naming of some combatants in the plays Cromwell and Bonaparte could not have happened until those figures made their appearance in the world. However, as far as play borrowings are concerned, the inclusion in mumming performances could have occurred as long as those plays were popular in fairground tressle or booth performances. And we have seen that most popular plays in the licensed theatres took on a longer life through adaptation in the fairground. It is not likely that rural communities saw the indoor theatre, but the fairground versions enjoyed the popularity of very large numbers of people. A Droll was made out of *Mucidorus* and this play is named as one of the Shropshire May-day entertainments performed by amateurs. The contemporary observers emphasize that the parts played were those where the Fool had the major role and the accidental advantage of pursuing the Fool's history is that certain parts of the larger jigsaw fall together of their own accord; partly because of his dominance and partly because of the fairground: a place of promiscuous entertainment where people who might never see a full-length play could be influenced by a shortened Fool Droll. The irate writer to *The Craftsman* in 1727, complaining of two Jack Puddings playing a Spaniard and an Englishman and allowing the Spaniard to knock down the Englishman, might have seen a fresh Droll, or this could have been a mumming play. The combat is not necessary to a Droll but is central in a mumming play. What is also important is the strange assortment of fairground people themselves who, according to Paterson, impressed their audiences by their bizarre appearance and properties. It is the fairground ingredient which is so far missing. One fact which seems indisputable is that the Jack Pudding who originally came from folk game saturnalia returned specifically as comic servant to the infallible folk doctor after Jack's association with the mountebank. In fact both characters were re-absorbed together.

For example, Richard Axton notes that the earliest, scripted folk games appear in *Mankind* (1460). In this play the Vices play the Fool and the time of year that the Morality play was performed was near the mumming season of today; 'structural motifs from the Christmas mummers' drama [occur] in the bizarre medley of the action' (p. 200). Among the sports is a demonstration of beheading and cure by Myscheff, without there being a servant there to supply comic banter. Most of the nineteenth-century texts do have this by-play. Further, the folklorist, Thomas Pettitt, notes several differences between the nineteenth-century doctor and the rest of the characters. 'In the matter of costume, for example, the Doctor is sometimes an idiosyncratic figure, invariably dressing as a Doctor. [He] often stands out as a naturalistic exception with his black coat, hat and bag. This visual idiosyncracy is matched by physical and verbal aspects of the Doctor's performance. Particularly revealing is the motivation of his entry, which is odd in being motivated at all' instead of complying with the formula of the rest of the play in which the characters present themselves as Lydgate wrote 'oon by oon'. Other aspects of the Doctor which Pettitt finds interesting are his relationship with his servant and their representational style of acting. He comes close to the historical evidence when he perceives that 'presumably, [this] imitates a kind of performance put on by the travelling quack doctors familiar from town squares and country markets'. Tiddy also pointed out that it is the scenes between the doctor and his servant, Jack, which provide the witty clowning and dialogue reminiscent of vaudeville patter. Pettitt concludes that 'just where the Doctor comes from is therefore a matter inviting speculation' (pp. 11-12). The evidence, however, is conclusive. The Doctor's character had changed from Myscheff's solo intervention, where his style does not differ from that of the other Vices, to an imitation of the mountebank and partner. The explicit evidence comes from a children's book of 1858, in which the black-hatted Doctor in their mumming play says 'I'm not like these little mountebank doctors that go about the streets, and say this, and that, and the other, and tell as many lies in one half hour as you would find true in seven years' (Yonge, p. 91). Of course the beauty of this declaration is that the denial confirms a connection in the mind of the audience. Naturalistic repartee between Doctor and servant is found in the one nineteenth-century example we have of mountebank and Fool patter in the 1820 children's book from Shropshire. As said in the last chapter, the Fool constantly deflates the mountebank's claims, and even his dignified poses. An example of the dialogue is as follows:

> Dr.   Why, sirrah do you never take physic?
> Andrew   Yes, master, sometimes.
> Dr.   What sort.
> Andrew   Any sort . . .
> Dr.   And how do you take it.
> Andrew   Why I take it . . . and put it on a shelf: and if I
>   don't get well again I take it down again and work
>   it off with a good strong ale.[1]

This compares well with the example Pettitt takes from the Western-sub-Edge play when the doctor calls Jack on to hold his horse. Jack asks:

> Will he bite?
> No.
> Will he kick?
> No.
> Take tow to hold him?
> No.
> Hold him yourself then.

The third specific fairground figure which I think was adopted by some mumming troups was the solo entertainer, described by Paterson as fighting his battle of life, industriously wandering from fair to fair with his show on his back. In several cases it is just such a character who does the begging at the end of the mummers' play. For example, at Burghclere, Johnny Jack comes in, with wife and family on his back, and makes his plea for money on the grounds of the difficulties of his life: 'the roads are dirty, my shoes are bad, so please put a little into my bag'. Speaight concludes that the man with the dolls on his back was Punch. In some cases this may be so, but there were alternatives. A nineteenth-century rhyme asked of a travelling Harlequin: 'To the fair do you carry a pack or a hunch/Are you mountebank, doctor or pedlar or Punch?' (Daniel, p. 201). In the Burghclere play it seems that the memory of such pathetic travellers, reduced to begging, was used as the most moving character to encourage generosity towards the mummers. As already said, the nickname for strollers became mummers and similarities between ragged travellers and seasonal, traditional players were striking. Fred Karno recalled that in about 1880, when he was with a poor travelling circus, members were compelled to imitate the mumming miners. They 'actually blacked their faces with soot, and, posing as miners, went around the neighbouring villages singing for coppers'.[2]

Then there is the remarkable set of verses which ends the 1700 *Harangues*. Under the heading 'The infallible Mountebank' is a mixture of sixteenth-century 'Vice' claims and lines which appear in every printed mumming text since. Firstly, the 'doctor rare/Who travels much at home' takes us back to the Vice and the line survives in the Ampleforth text: 'See, Sir, a doctor here, who travels much at home'. Secondly, the most intriguing group of verses is the following:

> I cure all ills,
> Past, present and to come;
> The Cramp, the Stitch,
> The Squirt, the Itch,
> The Gout, the Stone, the Pox;
> The Mulligrubs
> The Bonny Scrubs,
> And all *Pandora's* Box.

For one has to note that in the period *Mankind* was written there was another text, *The play of the Sacrament*, with a rhyming list of diseases and there are parallels with the later mountebank text. One, the earlier 'leche' comes from the Germanic area of Europe: his name is Master Brundyche of Brabant and two, the claims for cure are set in extensive rhyme. For example, 'the canker, the collick and the laxe/The tercian, the quartan, or the burning aches'. This interpolation has no affinities with folk ritual and (unlike the section from *Mankind*) reads like mountebank entertainment. The servant, Colle, enters first to praise his master but quickly drops the pretence to confide in the audience a comic list of the man's failings. Though the leach claims to be the greatest physician who ever saw urine, he is in fact near blind, has debts in every tavern, is lecherous and should be put in the stocks. Not only is there no reference to bringing the dead to life, but further Colle says to Brundyche's face that any man who feels well after his treatment must have died during it. But the Doctor section forms no part of the main action of the play: both master and servant play off the audience and therefore it would seem that this comedy was another popular theme in 'folk play'. There is no reference, either, to season, and emphasis is simply laid on the timeless jokes of the dangers inherent in using doctors. It is only in the rhyming diseases that the connection with folk play of chapbooks is found. There must have been a point when the mocked Doctor became incorporated into the mocked but magical Doctor of the mumming play and we have no pre-chapbook indication of when that was. The conclusion I come to is that whatever the mumming play prior to 1700 was, it was not as coherent in its text as it later became. After 1700 we see the death and revival remaining constant and, it seems to me, a wealth of characters from the fairground providing the comedy round the combatants. It is possible that the constant display of fairground humour helped to develop the mumming play up until the time when the texts began to be published.

During the sixteenth century the court had creamed off the best of the medieval mumming traditions which we know about and had incorporated them into the Masque. The one record we have shows that folk mumming was second-rate entertainment at a time when the Morris was still thriving. A northern gentleman, Nicholas Assheton, recorded the following visit to his father's house at Epiphany 1617/18: 'Twelfth-day. At night some company from Reead came a Mumming. was kindly taken: but they were but Mummers. Jan 7. Pack, rag, all away'.[3] Very briefly appears the suggestion that these mummers were disguised in the ragged costume which some troups still use; and the pack could either have been a reference to one character with a pack on his back, or the pack in which they carried their equipment. The lack of interest regarding their reception strongly contrasts with that given to the Morris in the same period. The suggestion that the country mumming was considered a debased form of entertainment in the 1600s comes also from two of Ben Jonson's masques; both written after he had accepted James I preference for the preliminary low-brow spectacle called the anti-masque. In *Christmas his Masque* (1616), Old Christmas leads in the ten entertainers who include personifications of Misrule and Mumming—the latter dressed 'in a masquing pied suit with a visor [mask], his torchbearer carrying the box and ringing it'. He is called a fishmonger and a knave who will win the medieval mumming game of dice instead of losing it in favour of his hosts. Such brief comments show Jonson's attitude towards the original custom. Further, Ancient Christmas reappears in some of the extant mumming texts and his cry on entry carries the sense of forceful entry contained in Jonson's line 'Ha! would you ha' kept me out'. Venus, who in the high Masque tradition should reform the ill-bred behaviour, appears as a deaf old lady known as Venus of Pudding Lane. Later, in 1622, Jonson wrote several anti-masques to precede the *Masque of Augurs*. The leader, Notch, is another low-life figure who has come to court because he heard court invention was at low ebb and he could fill the vacuum. He describes his offering as a 'disguise'; a word which horrifies the Groom of the Chamber since it is a word long-since discarded by men of taste. So country mumming still held an unhallowed place in society and, it seems, lay as a crude remnant stripped of its medieval dignity through the courtly borrowings and development into a magnificent art form of its own. And Jonson's reintroduction of the crude origins comes after that art form had itself degenerated. And it is a strange coincidence that all the seventeenth-century references to the Fool as Jack Pudding are placed in the context of either the Morris, the wooing game or the fair and never the mumming. This form of folk play seems to have become more fully developed later and it is possible that Jack Pudding and his companions revitalized the play, and the variegated fairground assembly became the subsidiary characters. It is always dangerous to put forward too strong a hypothesis, yet it is surprising to find so many characters in the printed mumming play with the name Jack and a strong predilection for pudding. To take a few examples, there is John Vinney from Weston-sub-Edge; Johnnie Jack from Burghclere; the Sapperton Jack Vinney; little Johnie Jack from Burlsdon; Little Saucy Jack from Cocking and the Ovingdean little Black Jack. Arbuthnot satirically makes pudding the central feature of English history. Addison, more directly, corroborates him. The people of Rochdale were known as harmless puddings, with the addition that all who went there thrived, save the indigenous people, which corresponds with the jibe that they were slow-witted. The late-nineteenth century comic-singers' scrap book sums up the Englishman with: 'The only thing that pleases and gives him relief/Is having lots of pudding and plenty of beef'. The phrase, 'of beef and pudding I'll have my fill' was used in a political ballad. Therefore, for many centuries beef and pudding persisted as the symbol for the average Englishman. And explicit association with mummers is found in a 1735 play, James Miller's *The Man of Taste*, where the foolery of Harlequin is preferred to that of native players:

> Maria   But come, Ladies, what say you of making a Party
> for the *French* Players? There's a charming Piece
> performed there To Night.
> Reynard Where our unpolish'd Beet-and-Pudding Clowns
> are so roasted.

At this date clown still meant the clumsy rustic, and the comment specifically brings in the common cry of the mumming players. To the gentry or anyone uninterested in mumming performances all the participants go by the name clown. They could all be called Jack Puddings – despite some variety of names – simply because the phrase in the text was usually spoken by one of the Jacks and beef and pudding were the staple rewards given to the mummers at Christmas. Curiously enough, London-based antiquarians, whose aim was to record British customs, had also lost touch with their contemporary traditions. John Doran wrote *Habits and Men* in 1854 and omits mention of any contemporary folk customs as he does in his later and more studied work, *The history of Court Fools* (1858). The book ends regretfully with Thomas Killigrew, although the history of Fools did not end in 1700. A late-nineteenth century *Scrap Book* contains verses which even include the continued custom of electing a Christmas King and Queen. The author calls the rhyme 'Christmas out of Town', since nobody now spends Christmas in town. He concludes that the genteel custom is so boring that he intends to be a 'nobody' and return to the old customs:

> In Billiter-lane, at this mirth-moving time,
> The lamplighter brought us his annual rhyme,
> The tricks of Grimaldi were sure to be seen,
> We carved a twelfth cake, and we drew king and queen;
> These pastimes gave oil to Time's round about wheel,
> Before we began to be growing genteel:
> 'Twas all very well for a cockney or clown [rustic]
> But nobody now spends his Christmas in Town.[4]

Le Roux and Garnier noted that even Crystal Palace entertainments were 'all noisy amusements which the society people avoid' (p. 46) and the inherited tricks of Grimaldi were finding greater appreciation in the rest of Europe. What is interesting is that, in retrospect, writers such as Sir Walter Scott in *Woodstock* and Besant and Rice in *The Chaplain of the Fleet* bring in a knowledge of Jack Pudding. Men acting the Fool in each book are reprimanded with the name and since both are historical novels it seems the authors were being historically correct and knew of the character, even though J.T. Smith lamented the dwindling presence of Jack Pudding's master, the mountebank, as early as 1815.[5] The great satirical magazine *Punch* was launched and, despite contributions from Thomas Hood, no mention of Jack Pudding or post-Grimaldi clowns was made. Even Joseph Strutt writes of most sports and pastimes in the past tense, although Henry Mayhew in *London labour and the London poor* (1851) finds it worthwhile to devote a chapter to festivities. These include Christmassing and Maying – the May now inevitable stolen from private land. The clowns are diverse: they include a sad clown; the Penny-Gaff clown (one-time Harlequin); the Canvas Clown and the Penny-Circus Jester (from large and small circuses) and, finally Silly Billy, who played the idiot. All these followed the Jack in the Green on May Day: a custom Roy Judge shows is related to the social changes in urban life.[6] In 1831 Isabel Hill shows the partiality for Jack in the Green, rather than for the May king or his clowns in verses published by Thomas Hood in his *Comic Annual*. Hill's poem makes up in detail for what it lacks in style.

A May-Day Vision

The masculine Marian – well painted – tho' ill it
Resembles a Lady well painted by Shee,
The Clown who exults as he holds up his skillet,
In motley and bells, raise no envy in me!
The King in court suit, and cocked hat of gilt paper,
May scrape me a bow, his fandangoes between,
But coldly I turn from his common-place caper,
To thy solemn measure – O Jack in the Green   [pp. 45-6]

In London some record remains of mummers' plays adapted for private performance at Christmas. For example, the one of 1858 already mentioned and one published in 1886 called *Christmas Revels or the Puritans discomfiture*. However, the only festivity vital enough to percolate through the metropolitan veil of respectability was the rapper-dance of north east England. In 1862 John Thrupp called it 'a sword-dance . . . a sort of sham-combat . . . the melodramatic combat which takes place at transpontine theatres at the present day, and in which the cuts and wards keep time to music'.[7] By 1890 the dance was assumed to be the Morris. *The Century Dictionary* (1889-1909) enters it as 'morris-dance – A kind of country-dance still popular in the north of England'.

In view of such alienation between London and the rest of rural England, it is clear that evidence for continuation of Fool customs lies in works written from outside the capital. Even the

American magazine, *Harper's* (1874, p. 192), provides a more accurate description of rural Easter gaiety than do London journals and the stimulus to look further comes from comments such as Charles Hardwick's, writing from Manchester. In *Traditions, Superstitions and Folk-Lore* he quotes the sixteenth-and seventeenth-century prohibitions on festive games but concludes 'the threat of excommunication and anathema failed to root them out of the heart of the mass of the population, and they survive to the present day' (p. 59). For the details we have to look elsewhere. Considerable new work is being done to bring these customs to light[8] and I shall attempt to use original sources, looking at the practices from the point of view of the development or survival of the Fool's role. It has to be said that there was considerable confusion from observers in different parts of the country as to what was Morris and what mumming and at times the two were combined. But it's still possible to see which is the southern Morris, which was northern guizing and which was the rapper-dance from the north-east. To begin with, Teresa Buckland has pointed out that many customs wavered on the point of extinction before the major revival at the beginning of this century and the information shows that the revivals were usually due to the vigour of one energetic town, which would send its team to the surrounding villages. Alun Howkins has researched the pre-Sharp material for Oxfordshire (where of course the Cotswold Morris was saved). Howkins' evidence continually shows how the fortunes of the dance fluctuated. The main tradition, dancing at Whitsuntide, is best found in the 1858 Whit Ale at Kirtlington. The whole festivity shows a surprising kinship with its sixteenth-century forbears, including the fact that the Fool had an uninhibited role to play. The main change was that the procession finished at the village green instead of the churchyard. On the green the Bowery was made; 'a shed made of green boughs . . . where the ale previously brewed was sold during the nine days of the feast without a licence. Also, a Lord of the Feast was elected and he, together with his mates, picked out a "Lady" who was paid for her services'. Ritual was included, for the Lord and Lady walked behind a man carrying a lamb: if possible the first-born of the season. It's probable that the lamb was part of the feast for its legs were formally tied together with pink and blue ribbon. The Lord carried the collecting box while behind him the Fool or Squire teased money from the spectators. The Fool's dress is described as motley and by the nineteenth century this could have meant many things. It was probably a patched dress with ribbons. The Fool carried the staff with bladder and cow's tail at opposite ends. 'His duties were to belabour the by-standers and to clear a ring for the dancers who followed him' (Howkins, p. 5). Exclusive male domination of the dance appears to have been a late decision. In about 1820 a set of women morris-dancers used to go out on Whit-Monday, and the Fool or Squire did not shrink from accompanying them. And in this century Tizzy Buckingham 'danced with Bampton on occasions, and was as good as any man', though she is not given the name of Maid Marion.

The neighbouring town of Spelsbury had the rival attraction of a spring fair, visited by booth performers. Despite this, the Morris remained one of the main features. Several teams tra-velled there to compete and collect money in much the same way as the Kingston games of 1509/10 travelled to neighbour-ing villages. We know that in the nineteenth century each team of the upper reaches of the Thames had its own recognized circuit and only visited each other's territory by arrangement. The Headington Morris (which prompted Cecil Sharp's interest when they played out of season during the hard winter of 1899) travelled to the City of Oxford and villages to the east. Kirtlington and Bampton kept to the west of Oxford. When Bampton was in decline it was the fiddler, Jinky Wells, who maintained the circuit with his solo performance. He would not have been aware of it, but the tradition he was force to follow was that of solo, jig-dancing fool. The Cotswold dance has become a feature of southern England again, thanks to Sharp's work, but it seems the Fool is more subdued than his ancestors and it is the dance which is now the centre of attention. Greater evidence that the nineteenth-century Fool was an uninhibited character comes from other writers: particularly Charlotte Burne's 1883 edition of Georgina Jackson's work on *Shropshire Folk-Lore*. The second compiler, who notes the number of varieties of Morris and mumming customs, was William

Sandys. However, Burne's work contains several points of value. Firstly, she was aware of the overlap in terminology in her county, where all winter visitors were known as Morris men (although the season is wrong) and the Easter seasonal play and outdoor stage plays were called mummings. Burne was aware that the confusion was due to the fact that Shropshire lies between the Morris country to the south and the combat drama of the north-east. She wrote:

> It seems as if no Midwinter feast in any country could be complete without its masquerade. In Shropshire we have two distinct varieties of these disguised and unbidden guests: the morris-dancers of South and West Shropshire, whose performance consists only of dancing and sometimes singing; and the so-called morris-dancers of the north-eastern quarter, in Staffordshire more accurately termed *guisers*.   [p. 410]

And it was in the guizing that the Fool or Fools played their large and riotous part. The mummers who came from Newport (on the borders of Staffordshire) were not only unbidden guests, but frequently unwelcome ones as well. If a householder heard their all-licensed behaviour in the street she would bar the door, otherwise 'in rushed a rabble rout of masquers without leave asked or given, and interlarded their performances with all sorts of antics and mischievous pranks'. Four characters appear to have adopted the Fool's part; Open-the-door – since that was what he did –; the widely travelled Doctor; Devil Dout, and the man in Fool's dress who was in the case of Newport called Billy Beelzebub. Some of the properties carried by the Fool are those which Sandys says the Old Father Christmas carried and the complete costume of Old Father Christmas was very much that of the medieval devil, Beelzebub. There was the calf-skin, the grotesque face and the club. In some seventeenth-century rhymes, 'Antient Christmas' is called to as though he were a yearly, visiting spirit and so the variation is not so great as it might seem. Fluidity of characters is part of the variety found throughout Britain, and since they all played Fools' parts, helps confirm that all the ancillary characters were varieties of Fool. In many texts the Fool protests that he is not Beelzebub although he carries the devil's properties and carries out his role. It is easy to see that the medieval association between devil and Fool had loosely remained, though it is doubtful that the relationship was understood. The Newport Fool wore a combination of insignia, 'white calico garments sewn all over with many-coloured bits of ribbon, etc. He has a bell fastened in the middle of his back, and . . . always carried a club in the left hand, and a long ladle . . . in the right' (p. 483). If you eat with the devil use a long spoon. The proverb may well have originated from the Fool/Devil's ladle. The other most interesting character in the Staffordshire masquerade was Little Devil Dout. As Chambers and Burne noted, the name comes from 'do out' or extinguish a fire. Burne records that when he threatened to sweep everyone into the grave he swept the grate, scattering dust and sticks until paid to desist. Ritual combat was between two characters only; King George and Singuy (a corruption of St Guy). These guizers' main purpose was a Fool riot, and when Sandys said, more decorously, that those characters who accompany the combatants but have nothing to do with the main action were 'burlesque characters' he confirms that some places were more interested in the burlesque than the combat. Burne mentions that Devil Dout was frequently omitted from the action, since his behaviour was the most threatening. The superstition remained that the hobgoblin intended to disturb the hearthside gods and bring bad luck on the house for the ensuing year.

In comparison, the southern morris-men were far more restrained. Though initially it seems surprising that the Oxfordshire teams were, in Shropshire, associated with winter, the explanation coincides with the very reason why Cecil Sharp saw the Headington team at all. Burne wrote that it was 'a common thing in hard winters for frozen-out bricklayers or quarrymen [and the Headington team were quarrymen] to get up a morris-dancing party, and dance in the streets of the neighbouring towns and villages to collect money' (p. 477). The Fool of the southern Morris sounds even more like Beelzebub. 'His face was blackened. He capered about independently of the rest, shrieked occasionally, and presented his collecting box to passers-by'. And Burne doesn't say what his dress was. That of Beelzebub would seem the most appropriate despite the winter weather. The southern Morris also made visits in its proper season at Whitsuntide; but it was not this sort of May game which had made itself traditional in Shropshire, but rather adaptations of fairground Drolls, performed by the local people. The Fool had his leading role and was expected to perform 'all manner of megrims ... going on with his manoeuvres all the time'. He was dressed as asinine forbears and had a mask, below a cap of hairskin with the ears up and bells at his knees. Some of the 'plays' mentioned have a history which goes back to the seventeenth century. The titles mentioned are *Prince Mucidorus, The Rigs (tricks) of the Time, St George and the Fiery Dragon, Valentine and Orson* and Mountford's comic adaptation of Marlowe's *Faustus*, now known as *Dr. Forster*. Only the second title does not appear in Rosenfeld's *Theatre of the London Fairs*. All the rest were well-known fairground drolls. Even *St. George and the Fiery Dragon* seems to have been based more on Fool-Droll than combat drama. 'Valiant St George and the Dragon, a farce' was popular in Bartholomew Fair as early as 1686 and provided the last unfortunate appearance by Elkanah Settle in his old age, when he played the dragon, 'thereby earning immortality in Pope's Dunciad'.[9] All these Drolls were farces and there is no reason for *The Rigs of the Time* to have been different. Shrewsbury had a fair which lasted until the late nineteenth century, and so we can't come to the tempting conclusion that the Maytime players had been using these Drolls for two centuries. They could have been performed at the fair some time after they had been written. However, the adoption of a Droll instead of the morris games for the main Whitsuntide celebrations shows just how far the interchange of ideas in the fairs could go. The Shropshire style of playing was just like early booth theatre as illustrated in the sixteenth century by the Flemish painter, Bruegel. 'The stage was erected on two wagons outside some building, usually in connection with a public-house, and was so arranged that the players as they made their exits passed into a sort of Green Room within the building itself, where they were regaled with cakes and ale whilst awaiting their next call. As a rule, no more than two players were on the boards at the same time, except in the final scene' (Burne, p. 494).

By comparison, Sandys tells us that mumming plays and

revised mumming plays for private performance, which he calls 'mock plays', were, in Cornwall, performed at Christmas. This is the time when you would expect them. Less emphasis was given to the Fool, who was one of the several 'burlesque' characters accompanying the main action. The leading Fool figure, dressed as the devil, was Old Father Christmas, 'personified as a grotesque old man, wearing a large mask and a wig, with a huge club in his hand'. A second comic character was the doctor and his dress was a cross between mountebank and white-faced clown. They called him 'a sort of Merry Andrew to the piece, is dressed in some ridiculous way, with a three-cornered hat and painted face'. Finally Sandys says that occasionally there was a female character, played by a woman; 'she' dressed in the costume of her great-grandmother.[10] The illustration in Sandys' later book[11] seems to be a reproduction of this description and shows that the combat aspect of the drama and not the riot was the focus of attention. The fighting men are elaborately dressed in the peaked hats worn by officers during the Napoleonic wars, and beribboned white shirts and trousers. In the drawing are three protagonists and as Sandys says, their costume is like that of the Morris-dancer. The texts Sandys gives contain no Jack Fool, and Father Christmas has the Fool's lines. The brief text is fleshed out in performance with four or five combats.

For Fools in seasonal playing, it seems we have to look further north. There is a further example from Shropshire which again seems to have been borrowed from processing strollers and circuses and had all but died out by 1882. All that was left of this 'ancient pageant' which made its way to the annual Shrewsbury Show was 'an advance guard of two burlesque characters, one with painted nose on a donkey, and the other on horseback dressed in red, and flourishing an immense cudgel, collecting coppers to cover the expense'. The mixture of circus and mumming clowning continued to cling to the dwindled remains of the people's holiday 'while showmen, who have come many a weary mile to attend it in former days, continue their rounds through the country, to pick up the crumbs of former pleasure fairs and show holidays!.[12] At the show professional performers and local amateur ones were on an equally low level. Curiously, the jesters at Knutsford's show were gaining popularity at this period and perform today, and I shall return to them at the end of the chapter.

In most parts of the country, even though the customs were different, the one thing which generally remained contant was the leadership of the Fool. This was probably the instinctive pattern since, as Paterson said, the clown or Fool was always the most popular character. In the thriving rapper-dance performances, which William Henderson observed in 1866 and which took place in most towns from the Humber to the Cheviot Hills, the 'old style' performance employed two clowns. In Durham alternative sets of verses had developed. Henderson records the old style with nine men, 'five dancers, one a clothes carrier, two clowns and one fiddler'. Despite the attraction in the skill of weaving the swords, the Fool behaved as the men's leader. All the talking was left to him and he introduced himself first with a lengthy monologue, which included the old claim of being widely travelled. The dancers paraded up and down until the Fool called them on, one by one. He had a stanza of description for each man, who held his sword upright and walked in a circular motion until all five had been called on in the same way and were marching in a ring. (The pattern is startlingly like that of the sixteenth-century *bouffons* or Fools' dance).[13] The leading Fool was called Tommy and wore animal head and skin. The second was the man/woman, Bessy. Henderson does not mention any mock beheading in the old Durham dance although the clown's verses are printed complete. And, in his description, the sword weaving and the knot are kept separate from any of the Fool's activities. However, since there was a male and female Fool, as in the Revesby play, it seems that in other versions mock-beheading of Tommy would have taken place since the Bessy presents the element of wooing competition. Other Fool activities in the north-east appear to have been less violent than those in Staffordshire, though this may have been Henderson's experience only. According to him, when the teams entered people's houses, the Fool cleaned the hearths to wish good luck for the New Year. Easter and Whitsuntide were sometimes occasions for the sword dancers to come out. But it was the Harvest Home which

was second in importance to Christmas, with guizing sometimes enjoyed after the Harvest Home supper.

Further south, in Lincolnshire, the dance described by
Washington Irving was not the rapper but a stave dance which
had more in common with Cotswold dancing. The costume was
that of the Morris and the Fool, though sporting his Beelzebub,
animal skin, had a lesser role. While the dancers performed the
stick dance 'advancing, retreating and striking their clubs together, keeping exact time to the music' the Fool capered round
the outside and rattled the Christmas box at the spectators. The
note of decorum in this performance may have been due to its
venue, which was at the house of the Squire of Bracebridge. The
out of season playing may also have been due to the special
invitation. Irving noticed traces of mockery among some of the
troup towards their host. 'It is true, I perceived two or three of
the younger peasants . . . when the squire's back was turned
making something of a grimace, and giving each other the wink'
(p. 88). And it may well have been ambivalent feelings towards
their benefactors which led to the alternative title of 'squire' to
many Fools. So it seems that some of the lack of communication
between antiquarians and rural customs may have been caused
by deliberate secrecy in the country. As early as 1759 a London
well-wisher went a few miles out of London to study the
pastimes of the folk and ended up being teased by the wenches
and rolled in a ditch by the swains.[14] At Bracebridge, the
servants were encouraged to keep up Christmas revelry 'provided everything was done comfortably to ancient usage'. They
were given twelve days of liberty but we are not told what
customs they kept. The squire and his family elected a Lord of
Misrule who organized a private mumming play, or, more
exactly, a masquerade. Known mumming characters from
summer and winter games were indiscriminately mixed, but
the Lord led the team as the new Fool character, Antient
Christmas. He was accompanied by Dame Mince Pie, Robin
Hood and Maid Marion. The most interesting contribution
was made by the children. They blackened their faces and came
as Roast Beef and Plum Pudding 'and other worthies celebrated
in ancient maskings'. And so it's clear that the real Christmas
mumming was known in Lincolnshire and the more mis-

chievous characters from the play were taken on by the children. For summer, the village of Bracebridge followed the pattern of Oxfordshire, particularly when a wedding took place. The one example Irving saw had an interesting interruption which indicates the changes in social values which were also helping to discourage the games from people of the class who had maintained the tradition. A man tried to stop the dancing 'decrying these idle nonsensical amusements in times of public distress'.[15]

The final bastion for Fool game-playing is, as is well-known, Cheshire, where the Antrobus mummers still go out at Christmas. At the other side of the country is the north Lincoln-shire Hood game at Haxey, which has been fully described by Christine Hole and, according to legend is a continuation of a thirteenth-century custom. It is an isolated phenomenon and seems to be a unique relic of a Fool-led football match, such as those drawn by Bruegel. Alex Helm shows that about thirty-three winter plays were still played in Cheshire at the turn of this century and since north-west England is a Roman Catholic stronghold this may account for Charles Hardwick's statement that neither *excommunication* nor anathema could prevent their continuation, although his own opinion was that they were based on pre-Christian games and this had of course been the reason for their prohibition. Helm's collection falls into three sections: twenty-six All-Souling plays, four Christmas plays, and three Easter plays. Helm perceptively noted that the apparent division in season is not itself important since it indicates the old tradition when the playing season itself ran from autumn to early spring. The lack of contemporary re-corded dating of the season when the play was seen emphasizes the conclusions of Alex Helm. The impression given is that the ones described were in fact seen at Easter. In 1859 Henry Green indicated that it was at Easter that he allowed into his house a performance which he believed derived from the medieval Mystery plays. The folk-play, called mock-heroic, was the basic one of St George and his various combatants. The play included a Fool who assured the audience he was not Beelzebub, despite his carrying the club and collecting ladle. There was also the Doctor giving a version of 'the itch, the stitch, the palsy and the gout' speech. Green's account is a little conservative and he quotes from the Rector of Bartlemy; who, in 1856, published letters to his son about the Cheshire Rectory. Despite being a clergyman, Hinchliffe is far more enthusiastic about what he saw. He was a frequent spectator and particularly appreciated the all-licensed Fool, who, Hinchliffe says, could make or break a performance. He wrote that the plays

> were sometimes with considerable humour; especially when the fool had a native talent for versification, and interlarded his part – not always marked by decency of language – with comical observations on the passing events of the neighbourhood which were quickly apprehended by the rustic or domestic audience, and hailed with peals of laughter. **(p. 143)**

Morris dances and their Fools are mentioned in passing, but the most popular event in Cheshire at Easter-time was the continuing performance of the combat drama which we normally associate with winter. The interesting result of this is that the Betley May game window, which was at that time in the possession of a local man, Mr Tollet, bore no resemblance to the May game practices he saw, though in earlier centuries it no doubt did. The window shows a May Lady, a Friar, two or three suitors two Morris dancers and a Fool. Mr Tollet wrote a full paragraph giving his 'opinion concerning the Morris Dancers upon his window' and stressed that the picture had no association with the Mayings which did take place in the county. (Hinchliffe, p. 193.)

There were other Fool customs in Cheshire. One was the electing of a Lord of Misrule by the men who dug out top dressing for farms from the side of the road. The men, called Marlers, had a 'lord of the pit' who collected money in summer from passers-by and proclaimed it in a parodic manner at the end of each day. The men made a ring and cried 'Oyez, oyez, oyez, Mr. – has this day given my lord and his men part of a hundred pounds'. Should the money be more than sixpence, the figure was raised to part of a thousand pounds. It isn't surprising that the nearest equivalent to this comes from the neighbouring county of Shropshire. Here, the election of a Lord

Marrall was part of the May games, and it may be more than coincidence that Arbuthnot used this name for his fool-ambassador in *The Gentleman's Magazine*. Other aspects of the Cheshire play – apart from the dominance of the winter play – which were unusual, were that at Easter girls sometimes played the male parts, and a Bessy from the Morris was included. In *Cheshire Gleanings* (1884) William Axon wrote that the Fool led the play and 'in addition to his other vocation' announced St George in a lofty strain. Devil Dout kept his threatening behaviour. It is said that the audience gave him money because 'his sweeping out was far too realistic to be pleasant' (Axon, p. 157). Helm's collection of plays shows almost no sign of Devil or Dairy Dout, which is a strange omission from the memories of those asked, and it is possible the gap was deliberate, since the character was the least civilized. The Antrobus Souling players expected ad libbing from the Doctor, Beelzebub and the Driver of the Hobby Horse, and Derry Dout is a very minor character with only a brief appearance. However, since the horse was another centre of attraction, where he appeared, and could take over the perogative of being threatening, the little Devil might not have been needed. All the ad libbing characters could act as Fools. And in Cheshire texts no servant appears with the Doctor. Like the mountebank of Bangor Bridge, it seems that the Doctor played the Fool himself.

Southern Lancashire also had Pace Egg Mummers, who blackened their faces and generally fought with any rival troups they might meet (even if they were out at Easter). The combat and the drama worked in two dimensions. The text which appears in *Lancashire Legends and Traditions* (1873) shows the vigour of the action and the humour. Charles Hardwick, the editor, states tht it was the Fool's 'byplay, antics, and buffeting of the spectators, especially women, with a bladder suspended to a stick [which served] to sustain the action of the piece throughout (p. 78). Rushbearing of course was the more important festival in many places and though the cart of rushes for the church was accompanied by a Morris and Fool (often a Bessy) the spectacle was not organized by the Fool. Usually the rush-bearing merged with a fair at the end of the day and there were more practised mountebanks and their Fools. Rushbearing was especially well organized in Rochdale, with competitions between several parishes. The gaiety and energy recorded makes one wonder how the phrase 'Rochdale puddings' ever came about.

It is possible that the authorities in Staffordshire, Cheshire and Lancashire disapproved of the near riot of the winter play and encouraged a more subdued celebration. The Shropshire festivities were actively discouraged, except for after the Harvest Home. And at Knutsford in Cheshire records for the May-day celebration, other than the combat play, begin in 1864. It existed before then, for Henry Green in the same book in which he mentions the ancient play also includes the Maypole and accompanying games at Knutsford. Again, Green is careful to emphasize the 'proper' and not the pagan side of the practice. The 'Christian may surely rejoice amid garlands and flowers, that a gracious Providence is again calling forth from the earth its various fruits for man' (p. 56). But the Knutsford practice of the May Queen and attendants included a wagon of Fools, and the celebration has not only survived to the present day but the extent of the games has grown. Though it is surprising to find such a survival, there are reasons. The Prince and Princess of Wales visited it in 1887 and Princess Mary patronized it in 1927. After 1887 Knutsford adopted the name 'Royal' for the day and for its jesters. In 1881, before the first royal visit, a reporter from *The Lancashire Figaro or Northern Charivari* visited it. The tone of his report was probably to suit the humorous style of the paper. The description is laconic and he praises the Morris dances alone; which suggests that though Morris dancing did not receive wide attention earlier in the century, it was, neverthess, regularly practised. The reporter does not even mention the jesters but a quarter of a page is devoted to an illustration of them in a horse-drawn wagon. The jesters themselves are in Fool's parti-colouring and the man leading the horse and the decorations, appear to have been influenced by the circus. Also, despite the reporter's deprecation the title page of the paper did, for a while afterwards, carry the picture of a Fool's head.

Extant programmes from 1907 show that the central features have remained the same and are worth mentioning for their historical continuity and also because one custom has been thought defunct. As well as the Royal jesters, Robin Hood and his men provide a play and the Jack in the Green, whose last appearance was thought to have been in the 1920s, follows immediately behind the local Morris troup. Today, the heartening aspect of the celebration is the introduction of dance troups (mainly Morris) from a wide area of Europe. It was Douglas Kennedy who said that customs change if they are to survive and the extension of Morris competition to Europe is the appropriate welcome change for today. But to conclude this summary of English Fool games – and those at Knutsford are perhaps more decorous than they were—the closest comparison with the sixteenth-century May procession comes from a pre-war programme:

> No account of Knutsford would be complete without a mention of the annual festival on the heath. The whole populace are *en fête* for the occasion, which is still a great attraction for miles around. A large procession is formed of hundreds of the local inhabitants in fancy dress, representing historical or fabulous characters, including King Canute [after whom Knutsford was named], Jack in the Green, and the Royal Jesters. The pricipal event is the crowning of the May Queen, attended by much ceremony, after which exhibitions of Morris dancing, old-world and modern dancing are given.   [1937]

The celebration is not without order and it is described from an opposite point of view to that of sixteenth-century opponents of games. Also, the Queen is the centre of attraction instead of presiding with the elected King over the attractions of energetic displays. The Fools keep up their antics: boys have now replaced the men and they are no longer in charge of the proceedings – for good or ill. For it appears that even in the nineteenth century and previous centuries the main Fool-led game was the mumming play. This statement is not meant to minimize the central action of the combat drama, but most observers comment on the talents of the Fools to hold the non-sequential series of entrances and actions together. With the old text of the rapper dance, the Fool was the only man who spoke. The contrast with Morris dancing is easy to understand. The dance itself is attractive spectacle whereas textual plays relied on those visited understanding the reason for the visit, and local gossip could be included to bring the audience into a close relationship with the performance. And so it isn't surprising that in our constantly-moving society mumming has all but disappeared. It needs a more static community, which could relate the ritual to the village's life as a whole even if, as in Shropshire, it was not always so welcome. The rough lines such as 'in comes I, *welcome or welcome not*' make sense in view of the riotous behaviour of the performers. The text clearly incorporated the intrusive nature of the mummers' appearance as a defiant joke.

Conclusion

The conclusion I have reached is that the Fool in cap and bell began his exploits in England earlier than previous evidence has shown, and that his existence persisted through a change of name over a longer period than previously thought. We have at least five centuries in which the Fool showed considerable tenacity and vigour. Whether or not his origins were in pre-Christian priestly ritual in Britain we do not know. The reasons for thinking so come from comparison with such rituals which took place in other countries, as for example the eastern, mystic Fool. Evidence for England begins with the Christian Church and the term 'fool' was used to describe the idiot, with whom churchmen had sympathy – directly, because of St Paul's Epistles – not antipathy for a cult figure they opposed. Opposition to pagan practices was concentrated on animal sacrifices and forms of bestial imitation and for some reason the term *stultus* was omitted from decretals on this subject. Opposition only began when the Church realized that an increasing number of men were earning their living by imitating the witless man. So by the time British evidence appears, the impression is that dressing in cap and bell by artificial and seasonal Fools was for entertainment and the expression of high spirits; only mock beheading in some rapper dances and the death and revival action of mumming plays suggests an original, deeper meaning. However, the gay dress of the Fool seems to have originated as an expression of celebration.¹ Therefore, the path trodden here has been that of entertainment and the evidence shown in context of theological or respectable opinion. And the English Fool was rarely appreciated by the respectable classes. Arguments for ritual ancestry came in the educated, nineteenth-century deductions: the Frazerian view based on anthropology which E.K. Chambers inherited. It is worth noting that original, sixteenth-century opposition to Fool-games was on the grounds that they descended from Roman saturnalia, which was a time of celebration without sacrifice. Having said that, many Morris dancers today say that whether they like it or not they do experience a sense of ritual when performing the dance. There is a fertility ritual behind it and when the hobby horse or the Fool picks out young girls in the audience to tease, there is a common belief that those girls will marry soon and produce children.

However, when we look back historically at the Fool's place in society, the evidence shows that he survived through wit and tricks: both arts of the entertainer. To be a professional Fool today does not depend on costume (apart from circus clowns) but on a high degree of individualistic talent and it would be necessary to write analytic biographies of individual comedians to pursue their Fool inheritance. Hollywood's silent films gave the Fool his greatest creative freedom this century, and many comic acts use the fundamental device of two men playing off one another –one clever, the other not. But compared with their medieval ancestors both are artificial, since the stooge uses the pretence of stupidity and sometimes turns the tables on his companion. One historical comparison exists in Skelton's *Magnyfycence* (*c* 1530), where two Fools, who act as Vices, plot the downfall of Magnyfycence, but when together they have a scene where one is stupid and the other clever. The Vice/Fool is especially interesting. He was closely associated with the devil and some lines from sixteenth-century Vices occur in mumming plays. It seems very likely that Morality playwrights replaced the undisciplined Fool and Devil in folk play – such as the by-play in the Hell scenes of Mystery *Cycles* – with a means of teaching eventual sobriety. Textual comparisons between scripted comedies and printed folk plays have been made by R.J.E. Tiddy and E.K. Chambers, and long before this comment had been made on the interrelation between the amateur and professional Fool. John Jackson observed that as a boy (about 1740) he first saw 'in a remote part of England one of those sets of irregulars . . . called *mummers*; from which appellation that outré mode of playing commonly practiced by itinerant actors, and sometimes even upon the established

Theatres, is, we presume, stiled mumming'. Jackson also adds that in his time the Fool was not only the presenter of the rapper dance, but that he added various tricks: 'after being tumbled about in different positions [he] frightened his companions from the stage, which closed the scene'. This conclusion turns the tables on the appearance that the mock-beheaded Fool remains the comically-helpless scapegoat. Jackson concludes, at a period which we might call an *early* one for folk play scholarship, 'while it would be rash, at this late stage of scholarship, to assert that folk drama derives from the medieval or Elizabethan theatre, *it is clear that folk drama, "village theater", and the regular drama and travelling players . . . participated in an intense interaction*'[2] (my italics). Jackson's dates coincide with the period when successful comedians were attempting to disassociate themselves from the exaggerated or outré behaviour described and which had been so successfully practised by Joe Haines. However, outré is the word used by Dibdin to describe the successful pre-Grimaldi clown up to and including Dubois and in view of Jackson's experience the rustic appearance of these clowns would seem to have been in direct imitation of mumming Fools. The time for reciprocal borrowing was after Grimaldi's inspiration. The Cornwall mumming doctor, shown by Sandys, whitened his face. And it was Grimaldi-styled clowns who thereafter followed in London May games. It is strange to find that J.T. Smith's nostalgia for the old and rumbustious fairground Jack Pudding was not transferred to the changed Fools. In *Vagabondiana* he protested that 'now, instead of . . . innocent May-day gaiety the streets are infested by such fellows as the one exhibited in the adjoining plate [one of Mayhew's street-clowns][3] who have been dismissed, perhaps for their indecent conduct, from the public places of entertainment. These men hire old dresses, and join the Chimney Sweeper's Cinder-sifters, or Bunter's Garland, or Jack in the Green &c. and exhibit all sorts of grimace and ribaldry to extort money from their numerous admirers' (p. 40).

It's worth concluding with one or two other opposite viewpoints. In 1859 Eliza Cook expressed her pleasure at returning to London for Christmas because of the games; indoors and out.[4] Her attitude is supported by the man from Billiter Lane and by drawings in the *Illustrated London News* (1842, p. 548) where the King and queen are plump monarchs of the cake and the Fool has all the insignia accumulated by the nineteenth century: a Grimaldi face, hood with ears, parti-coloured dress and a bladder on a stick. *The Graphic Christmas Number* (1879) shows a parti-coloured Fool examining an empty flagon of wine with the caption 'Though lost to sight to memory dear'. However, in an earlier illustration in the *Comic Magazine* (1833, p. 280) we find a splendidly depicted *lack* of welcome for the poor mumming Fool. The amateur, seasonal entertainer is dressed in Fool's cap, bib, Grimaldi face and ribbons at his knees. With his broom by his side he sits in defeat upon a barrel. Over him stands a genuine Devil Dout of a child, grimacing; and it is clear that the rope tying the Fool's ankles together is the lad's work. It is not surprising if the traditional play kept to rural confines and slipped from the knowledge of the metropolis until F.T. Ordish began the series of textual discoveries at the end of the century, immediately before the demise of mumming foolery in most parts of the country.

Notes

CHAPTER 1

1 Doran, chapter 1.
2 Axton, p. 11.
3 Davis, *Past and Present*, p. 47.
4 Axton, *loc. cit.*
5 *Preterea sciendum est quod in multis locis prava est consuetudo ubi conveniunt in festivitate alicuius sancti lascive mulieres et stulti adolescentes et tota nocte cantant in cemeteriis et in ecclesiis lascivas et diabolicas cantilenas, ducendo ibi choreas suas et multos alios turpes ludos exercando. Omnia talia cum magna diligentia prohibenda sunt, si fieri potest. Sustinetur tamen in quibusdam locis, quia aliter non venirent multi homines ad tales festivitates nisi possent ludere.* (Thomas of Chobham, p. 292).
6 PRO SP 1.101, p. 33. Cf. Stubbes.
7 *In die etiam Circumcisionis Domini subdiaconis, et clericis de secunda forma . . . antiqua consuetudine immo verius corrupta regis stultorum ecclesiam et extra hactenus usita sublata penitus et extirpa.* (Dugdale, vol. 6, p. 1310).
8 Described by Mr. G.P. Brown of the Humberside County Council.
9 *The medieval stage.*
10 *Dicit quod subtrahuntur ipso expense per eum facte pascendo ly ffolcfeste in vltimo Natali, quod non erat propria, nec in cursu sed tamen rogatus fecit cum promisso sibi facto de effusione expensarum et non sibi satisfactum.* (*Lincoln Statutes*, pt. 2 (Cambridge, 1897) p. 388).
11 Exeter College, Oxford, MS 42, fol. 12r.
12 Septuagint numeration: Psalms 13 and 52. After 1547, numeration changed to 14 and 53.
13 Lucy Freeman Sandler.
14 In some cases the bauble resembles an orchid root, which was named after the male gender. One specie of orchid is named *orchis morio*.
15 *Ipsi credent se bene indutos & ornatus, eum equuseorum scilic corpus . . . cum tamen omnino nudi sint . . . Ipsi similes cuidam clerico qui in festo stultorum induit equum scarleto, & ipso indutus matta.* (Peraldus, p. 198).
16 Bullock-Davis, p. 67.
17 'fface vnstable, gasyng Est and South,
With loude lauhtres entrith his language
gapeth as a rook, abrood goth jowe and mouth
lyk as a iay enfomyned in hys cage. (Bodl. MS Laud. 683, ll 41-4).
18 'The tenthe fooll may hoppe vpon the rynge

Foote al aforn, and lede of riht the daunce. (Ibid., ll 25-6).

19 It is no game with wyves for to pleye
But for foolis [and such] with his rebeke may sing ful offt ellas!
Lyke as þeos hynes here stonding oon by oon
He may with hem vpon þe daunce goon   *i demonstrando vi rusticos* (Trinity College, Cambridge MS R.3.20, pp. 40-2).

20 Billington, 'Routs and reyes'.

21 Then all assembled for the game, and all the minstrels blew their pipes together and played for the shepherds, cowherds and swineherds to dance merrily to. 'Copyn Cull' could mean silly head: 'cop' from '*kopf*', and 'cull' from cully, which with cuddy was interchanged to mean simpleton. (*Bannatyne* MS vol. 4).

22 G.F. Jones, *Wittenwiler's ring and the anonymous Scots poem Colkelbie Sow* (New York, 1956) and E.F. Guy, *Some comic and burlesque poems in two sixteenth-century Scottish MS anthologies*, Ph.D. thesis (Edinburgh, 1952).

23 Swain, chapter 2.

24 . . . party hosen . . . pykede schone
Of fytered fitted clopes as foles done. (*Instructions for parish priests*, ll 1143-6).

25 See Nicols and Gilchrist for comparable Fool illustrations.

26 *Ibid.*

27 Billington, 'Sixteenth-century drama in St. John's College'.

CHAPTER 2

1 *Quis quod stultum est Dei, sapientibus est hominibus: et quod infirmum est Dei, fortius est hominibus.* (1 Corinthians, 2, verse 25).

2 *Puto enim quod Deus nos Apostolos novissimos ostendit, tanquam morti destinatos: quia spectaculum facti summus mundo, et Angelis, et hominibus. Nos stulti propter Christum.*

3 The German for Fool is used as the opposite of *tam* here.

4 Professor Dov Noy, The Hebrew University of Jerusalem.

5 John Saward, 'The fool for Christ's sake in Monasticism, east and west', *Theology and Prayer*, 3 (1975), pp. 29-55.

6 *The 1st Prayer-book of Edward VI, 1547, Everyman Series*, undated.

7 Nick Davis, *The playing of Miracles between circa 1350 and the Reformation*, Ph. D. thesis (Cambridge, 1977).

8 T.E. Allison, 'The Paternoster play and the origin of the Vices', *Publications of the modern language association*, 39 (1924), pp. 789-804.

9 *Domus talis est corpus hominis, Vix enim staret per quinque dies, nisi cibis & potibus fulciretur. Vnde irridendi sunt qui vanis ornatos illud depingunt. Et sicut ridiculum esset si loripes pedem ligneum depingeret, vel deaueret: sic ridiculum est cum homines se ornant. Tertio ostenditur per hoc, quod ornantes se mendicant pulchritudinem suam a creaturis vilioribus quam ipsi sunt. Nobilis homo embesceret a vilibus hominibus mendicare, & potius indigentiam sustineret, quam mendicaret ab eis: sic debet homo erubescere a verminibus & muribus suum mendicare decorem. (De Virtutibus ac Vitiis*, p. 198).

10 Bloomfield, p. 188.

11 Ac in fauntes ne in folis þe fend haþ no mi3t
  For no werk þat þai erche, wykkide oþer ellis [64-5]
12 þo þat feynen hem foolis and with faityng libbeþ . . .
  Thei konne na more mynstralcie ne Musik, men to glade,
  Than Munde þe Millere . . .   [39-45]
13 flateris and fooles arn þe fendes disciples
  To entice men þoru3 hir tales to synne and harlotrie. [429–30]
14 flateris and fooles þoru3 hir foule wordes
  Leden þo þ at liþed hem to Luciferes feste . . .
  Thus haukyn þe Actif man hadde ysoiled his cote
  Til Conscience acouped him þerof in a curteis manere   [454-8]
15 '. . . the Hawkins of the world are doomed to wear their filthy rags unless
  the spirit of Piers may be revived.' D.W. Robertson and D.F. Huppe, *Piers
  Plowman and Scriptural tradition* (London, 1951), p. 176.
16 Davis, *Society and culture in early modern Fran₂*.
17 *Miror de fasto tuo quod cum continua lectione defatigeris innumerabiles libros
  lectitando nondum ad humilitatem ductus sis hoc certe ex eo quia scientia huius mundi
  . . . stultitia quedam est apud deum, et hinc inflat, vera autem scientia humilat.*
  (Wilpert, ed. vol. 1, p. 216).
18 The chiefest man is he . . . that can find out the fondest kind of playes.
  On him they looke and gaze vpon, and laugh with lustie cheare,
  Whom boyes do follow, crying foole, and such like other geare. (Furnivall,
  ed. Stubbes, appendix, II 289-92).
19 Mak roume sirs how, that I may rin
  Lo, se quhair I am new cum in
    Begaryit all with sindrie hewis . . .
  Quhat say 3e sirs am I nocht gay?
    Se 3e not Flatterie, 3our awin fuil,
  That 3eid to mak this new array?
    Was I not heir with 3ow at 3ule? (Hamer, ed. vol. 2, ll. 602-10).
20 The game appears in *Wisdom that is Christ* at the nadir of Mynde's fall, and
  in Wager's, *The longer thou livest the more Fool thou art*, where with a cast of
  four effort is made to create the illusion of seven. See p. 45.
21 Hotson, *passim*.
22 A. and G. Feuillerat, eds. p. 98.
23 *Adstabat forte parasitus quidem, qui uideri uolebat initari morionem, sed ita
  simulabat, ut proprior uero esset, tam frigidia dicta captana risum, ut ipse saepius,
  quam dicta sua rideretur.* (E. Surtz and J.H. Hexter, eds. *The complete works of
  St. Thomas More*, vol. 4 (New Haven, 1965) p. 80).
24 *Chresteleros*, Book 6, epigram 39
25 J.O. Halliwell, ed. *Tarlton's jests and newes out of Purgatorie, Shakespeare Society*
  (London, 1844) p. xv.
26 *The collected works*, vol. 1, 'Newes out of Purgatorie', introduction.
27 *Ibid.*, 'Qvips vpon Qvestion', fol B.4.v.

CHAPTER 3

1 Anglo, 'Court festivals of Henry VII', p. 15.
2 Thomas, p. 7
3 Armin, 'Foole vpon Foole', fol. B.3.v.
4 E.B. White, ed. *The Eclogues of Alexander Barclay, Early English Text Society* (London, 1928) p. 10.
5 Billington 'Routs and reyes'.
6 Hobhouse, *Churchwardens' accounts.*
7 Kingston KG/12/1, pp. 16-66.
8 J.J. Johnson, ed.
9 PRO SP 1.1. fol. 33r.
10 Welsford, p. 212. Cf. Feuillerat, p. 98.
11 F.S. Boas, ed. *The Christmas Prince, Malone Society Reprints* (Oxford, 1923) p. 28.
12 Commissary Court, Cambridge, 7 September, 1638, MS 1.9, fol. 194v. Found by Dr Alan Nelson.
13 'Of watches of London', p. 101.
14 F.P. Wilson ed. *Malone Society Collections III* (Oxford, 1954) p. 10
15 Baskervill, p. 93.
16 Armin, ed. Feather, *Tayton's jests and the Newes out of Purgatorie*, p. 2.
17 'Tarlton's jig of a horseload of fooles' is generally thought to be a forgery by J. Payne Collier. However, I agree with Baskervill that it may have been sung and danced by Tarlton.
18 Sisson, p. 126, 128.
19 Mark Benbow, ed. Line 1065.
20 A political version of the Solomon/Marcolf theme. Swain, chapter 2.
21 'Wits miserie and the worlds madness', *The complete works of Thomas Lodge*, E.W. Gosse, ed. vol. 4 (New York, 1963) p. 84.
22 *Tudor facsimile texts* (London, 1912) Farmer ed. fol. 12r.
23 Armin, ed. Feather, fol. A.3v.

CHAPTER 4

1 Dunbar, pp. 261-2
2 *Pierce's supperogation* (1593) p. 47.
3 R.E. Latham, ed. *Revised Latin word-list* (London, 1965).
4 A. Thorndike, ed. *The minor Elizabethan drama* (Everyman series London, 1910) p. 40.
5 'The return of Pasqvill', Nashe, vol. 1, p. 83. Cf. Sisson, p. 161.
6 See Sandys, Burne and Green.
7 And 'untill the sad Catastrophe shews the Play to be a jig, all mockery and

Mirth . . . Sancho's a Player, and Acts a Lord'. (*Festiovs notes vpon Don Quixot*, Book 4, pp. 186-7).

8 *Quarter Sessions Rolls, Staffordshire, Michaelmas, 1655*, no. 23. Found by Barbara Lowe.

9 H. Stocks, ed. *Records of the Borough of Leicester 1603-88* (Cambridge, 1923) p. 232.

10 Bentley, vol. 6, p. 171.

11 *Ibid*, Bentley asks, 'was Jack Pudding a stage name?'.

12 J.P. Malcolm, ed. *Miscellaneous anecdotes illustrative of the Manners and History of Europe during the reigns of Charles II, James II, William and Queen Anne* (London, 1808) pp. 148-9.

13 Bentley, vol. 6, p. 171.

14 M. Lefkowitz, ed. *Trois Masques a la cour de Charles 1er d'Angleterre* (Paris, 1970) pp. 171-243.

15 E.S. de Beer, ed. *The diary of John Evelyn*, vol. 3, p. 253.

16 'The word Mountebanke (being in the Italian . . . *Monta'in banco*) is compounded of *Montare* . . . to ascend or go vp to a place . . . *banco* a bench because the fellowes doe act their part vpon a stage which is compacted of benches or fourmes, though I haue seene some fewe of them . . . stand upon the ground when they tell their tales . . . . such are commonly called *Ciaratones* or *Ciarlatans* . . . Twice a day, that is, in the morning and in the afternoone, you may see fiue or sixe severall stages erected for them: those that act vpon the ground, euen the foresaid *Ciarlatans* being of the poorer sort'. (Coryate, 1611) pp. 272-3.

17 *Philosophical Cellections* 3 (1681) pp. 48-50.

18 Smith, *Ancient topography of London*, p. 43.

19 18 April, no. 48.

20 'Thomas Marchant's diary', *Sussex Archaeological Society Publications* 25 (1873) p. 182.

21 *The Gentleman's Magazine* (1735) *passim*.

22 The continued popularity of this play shows in Hogarth's satirical print, 'Masquerade'. 1723-24, and in later Shropshire May Games. Dr Foster of the Gloucester nursery rhyme may have come from this itinerant version.

23 *Harangues or speeches of several famous Mountebanks in town and country* (London *c* 1700, reprinted 1762).

24 Rosenfeld, p. 136.

25 John Downes, *Roscius Anglicanus* (1671) p. 32.

26 Macaulay, vol. 2, pp. 195-6.

27 E. Adeler and C. West, *Remember Fred Karno* (London, 1939) p. 42.

28 *Amusant le Pont-neuf de ces somettes fades,*
    Aux Laquais assemblez, jouer ses Mascarades. (Boileau, ed. Schelts, Amsterdam, 1713).
    But for a tedious Droll a Quibbling Fool
    Who with low nauseous Baudry fills his Plays;
    Let him be gone and on two Tressels raise
    Some *Smithfield* Stage, where he may act his pranks,
    And make Jack-puddings speak to Mountebanks. (Collier quoting Dry-

den and Soames' translation).
29 Rosenfeld, p. 63.

CHAPTER 5

1 *Satyre on the Follies of Men*, p. 48.
2 *Merry Andrew's Epistle to his Old Master Benjamin, a Mountebank at Bangor-Bridge*, p. 9.
    The Shepherd's Week, 1711 p. 58.
4 Rosenfeld, p. 22.
5 'The droll players' lamentation', Daniel, vol. 1, p. 114.
6 *Ibid.*, p. 195.
7 Quack doctors appear in a farce called *Squire Trelooby* which was performed at Lincoln's Inn theatre on 30 March 1704.
8 *Elizabethan grotesque* (London, 1981).
9 Quoted in *The Gentleman's Magazine*, 1735, pp. 318-20.
10 *Ibid.*, (1738), pp. 295 & 414.
11 A death near Bath was reported in *The Daily Gazetteer*, Tuesday 27 August, 1745.
12 Pudding is Pudding still, they know
    Whether it has a Plumb or no;
    So, tho' the Preacher has no skill,
    A *Sermon* is a *Sermon* still. (Even Lloyd, 1766).
13 Morley, p. 385, illustration.

CHAPTER 6

1 *The Merry Andrew or, the Humours of a fair*, p. 5.
2 Charles Dibdin, senior, pp. 77-8.
3 *Ibid.*
4 *The Diary of Thomas Turner of East Hoathly 1754-65*, F.M. Turner, ed. (London, 1925) pp. 30-1.
5 Earwater, p. 571.
6 *Monthly Magazine* (1798) p. 416.
7 Willson Disher, p. 80.
8 Charles Dibdin Junior, p. 47.
9 Daniel, vol. 2, p. 7.

CHAPTER 7

1 *The Merry Andrew, or the Humours of a fair*, p. 17.
2 Adeler and West, *Remember Fred Karno*, p. 42.
3 'The journal of Nicholas Assheton of Downham in the County of Lancaster', *Chetham Society*, vol. 7 (Manchester, 1848) p. 74.
4 *The scrap book of literary varieties* (London, 1831), p. 63.
5 *Ancient Topography of London*, p. 21.

6 *Jack in the Green* (Ipswich, 1979).
7 *Anglo-Saxon England*, p. 385.
8 See *Roomer* and *Transmission*: publications of The Centre for English Cultural Tradition and Language, Sheffield University.
9 Rosenfeld p. 20.
10 *Christmas Carols*, 1833 p. lxi.
11 *Christmastide*, 1852 p. 145.
12 *Salopian shreds and patches*, see bibliography pp. 189-90.
13 T. Arbeau, *Orchesography*, Julia Sutton, ed. (New York, 1967).
14 *The Idler*, no. 71 (1759) p. 87.
15 Irving, pp. 45-117.

CONCLUSION

1 Billington, 'Routs and reyes'.
2 Jackson, pp. 409-11.
3 Reproduced in Judge, p. 16.
4 Cook, 'Home for the holidays'.

Bibliography

Adeler, E. and West, C., *Remember Fred Karno* (London, 1939).

Allison, T.E. 'The Paternoster play and the origin of the Vices', *P.M.L.A.*, 39 (1924) pp. 789-804.

Anglo, Sidney, 'The court revels of Henry VII', *Bulletin of the John Rylands Library*, 43 (1960-61) pp. 12-45.

Armin, Robert, *The collected works*, J.P. Feather, ed. 2 vols. (London, 1972).

Armin, Robert, *Tarlton's jests and the newes out of Purgatorie*, J.D. Halliwell, ed. *Shakespeare Society* (1844).

Arbuthnot, John, *The Crown-Inn satires* (London, 1717).

Arbuthnot, John (attributed), *The Dumpleid, or a learned dissertation on Dumpling* (London, 1726).

Ashton, John, *A century of ballads illustrative of the life, manners and habits of the English nation during the seventeenth century* (London, 1887).

Assheton, John, *The Journal of Nicholas Assheton, Chetham Society Publications*, 14 (Manchester, 1848).

Avery, E.L. 'Foreign performers in the London theaters in the early eighteenth century', *P.Q.* 16 (1937)) pp. 105-23.

Avery, E.L. 'Dancing and pantomime on the English stage, 1700-1737', *S.P.* 31 (1934) pp. 417-52.

Avery, E.L. *The London stage 1660-1800* (Carbondale, Illinois, 1960).

Axon, William, *Cheshire gleanings* (Manchester, 1884).

Axton, Richard, *European drama of the early middle ages* (London, 1974).

Bannatyne, George, *The Bannatyne manuscript written in tyme of pest 1568*, W. Tod Ritchie, ed. 4 vols. (Edinburgh, 1930-4).

Barber, C.L. *Shakespeare's festive comedy* (Princeton University press, 1959).

Baskervill, C.R. *The Elizabethan jig* (New York, 1965).

Bastard, Thomas, *Chrestoleros* (London, 1598).

Bellamy, Thomas, *The life of Mr. William Persons, comedian* (London, 1795).

Bentley, G.E. *The Jacobean and Caroline stage*, 7 vols. (Oxford, 1941-68).

Billington, Sandra, 'Routs and reyes', *Folklore*, 89 (1978) pp. 184-200.

Billington, Sandra, 'Sixteenth'century drama in St. John's College, Cambridge', *Reviews of English studies*, 29 (1978) pp. 1-10.

Bloomfield, M.W. *The seven deadly sins* (East Lansing, Michigan, 1952).

Boas, F.S. *University drama in the Tudor age* (Oxford, 1914).

Brand, John, *Observations on popular antiquities* (London, 1777).

Brice, Andrew, *Mobiad* (London, 1770).

Buckland, Teresa, ed. *The proceedings of the traditional dance conference*, vol. 1 (Crewe and Alsager College, 1982).

Bullock-Davies, Constance, *Menestrellorum multitudo: minstrels at a royal feast* (Cardiff, 1978).

Burne, Charlotte and Jackson, Georgina, *Shropshire folklore; a sheaf of gleanings* (London, 1883).

Butler, Samuel, *Characters* (London, 1665), C.W. Davies ed. (London, 1970).

Butler, Samuel *Vpon critics who judge of modern plays precisely by the rules of the antients* (c 1670).

Carrington, F.A. ed. *Wiltshire Archaeological magazine* (1854).

Cassell, William, ed. *The illustrated Shakespeare* (London, 1864).

Cawley, A.C. ed. *The Wakefield pageants in the Townley Cycle* (Manchester University press, 1958).

Chambers, E.K. *The medieval stage*, 2 vols. (Oxford, 1903).

Chambers, E.K. *The Elizabethan stage*, 4 vols. (Oxford, 1923).

Chambers, E.K. *The English folk play* (Oxford, 1933).

Chambers, R.W. *The book of days*, 2 vols. (London, 1863).

Chaucer, Geoffrey, *The works of Geoffrey Chaucer*, F.N. Robinson ed. (Oxford, 1957).

Chetwood, W.R. *A general history of the stage* (London, 1749).

Christmas revels or the Puritans discomfiture (London, 1886).

Comic magazine, The (London, 1833).

Concanen, Alfred (illustrator), *The Jovial Christmas* (London, 1880).

Cook, Eliza, *Poems* (London, 1859).

Coryate, Thomas, *Crudities* (London, 1611).

Croft-Cook, R. and Cotes, P., *Circus: a world history* (London, 1976).

Daily Gazetteer, The (1740-50).

Daniel, George, *Merrie England in the olden time*, 2 vols. (London, 1842).

Davis, Natalie Zeman, *Society and culture in early modern Europe* (London, 1975).

Davis, Natalie Zeman, 'The reason of misrule: youth groups and charivaris in sixteenth-century France', *Past and Present*, 50 (1971), pp. 41-75.

Dawson, W.F. *Christmas, its origins and associations* (London, 1902).

De Beer, E.S. ed. *The diary of John Evelyn* (Oxford, 1955).

De la Bère, ed. *John Heywood: entertainer* (London, 1937).

Dibdin, Charles (senior), *The Musical Tour of Mr DIBDIN; in which —previous to his embarkation for India—he finished his career AS A PUBLIC CHARACTER* (Sheffield, 1788).

Dibdin, Charles (Junior), *Professional and literary memoirs of Charles Dibdin the younger*, G. Speaight, ed. (London, 1956).

Dibdin, Thomas, *Reminiscencies of Thomas Dibdin* (London, 1827).

Dickens, Charles, ed. *The memoirs of Joseph Grimaldi* (London, 1838).

Dickens, Charles, *Sketches by Boz* (London, 1836).

Disher, M. Willson, *Clowns and Pantomimes* (London, 1925).

Ditchfield, P.H. *Old English customs* (London 1896).

Doran, John, *Habits and Men* (London, 1854).

Doran, John, *A history of court fools* (London, 1855).

Doutrepont, G. *L'Évolution du type de Pierrot dans la litterature française* (Brussels, 1925).

Dugdale, William, *Monasticon Anglicorum*, vol. 6 (London, 1846).

Dunbar, William, *The poems of William Dunbar*, J. Small ed. vol. 2 (Edinburgh, 1893).

Earwater, J.P. *East Cheshire* (London, 1880).

Egan, Pierce, *The life of an actor* (London, 1825).

Egan, Pierce, *The book of sports* (London, 1831).

Elson, J.J., ed. *The wits: or sport upon sport* (New York, 1932).

Erasmus, Desiderius, *Moriae Encomium* (Basle, 1515).

Evelyn, John, *The diary of John Evelyn:* see De Beer, ed.

Felver, C.S. *Robert Armin: Shakespeare's fool* (Kent State University Bulletin, Kent, Ohio, 1961).

Feuillerat, A & G. eds. *Documents relating to the revels at court in the time of King Edward VI and Queen Mary* (Louvain, 1914).

Fielding, Henry, *The Covent Garden Journal*, 10 (1752).

Fielding, Henry, *Pasquin* (London, 1736).

Findlater, Richard, *Grimaldi: king of clowns* (London, 1955).

Fournel, V., *Les spectacles populaires* (Paris, 1863).

Frost, Thomas, *Circus life and circus celebrities* (London, 1875).

Gay, John, *Fables* (London, 1732).

Gentleman's magazine, The, (1735-1820).

Gilchrist, A.G. 'A carved morris-dance panel from Lancaster Castle', *J.E.F.D. & S.S.* 1 (1933) p. 86.

Gildon, Charles, *The life of Thomas Betterton* (London, 1710).

Granger, John, *A biographical history of England from Egbert the great to the revolution* 6 vols. (London, 1824).

Green, Henry, *Knutsford: its history and traditions* (Manchester, 1859).

Halle, Edward, *Chronicle: containing the history of England, during the reign of Henry the fourth . . . to the end of the reign of Henry the eighth*, J. Johnson, ed. (London, 1809).

Halliday, Andrew, *Comical fellows: or the history and mystery of the pantomime* (London, 1863).

Happé, Peter, 'The Vice and the folk-drama', *Folklore*, 75 (1964) pp. 161-93.

Hardwick, Charles, *Traditions, superstitions and folklore* (Manchester, (1872).

Harland, J. and Wilkinson, J.T., eds. *Legends and traditions of Lancashire* (London, 1873).

Helm, Alex, *Cheshire folk drama* (The Guizer press, 1968).

Henderson, William, *Folk lore of the northern counties of England* (London, 1866).

Hinchliffe, E., Rector of Mucklestone, *Barthomley: letters of a former Rector to his eldest son* (London, 1856).

Hobhouse, E. ed. *Churchwardens' accounts of Croscombe, Pilton, Yatton, Tintinhull, Morebath, and St. Michael's; Bath, 1349-1560.* (Somerset record society publication, 1890).

Hole, Christina, *British folk customs* (London, 1976).

Hood, Thomas, *The comic annual* (1831).

Hornstein, L.M., 'King Robert of Sicily: analogues and origins', *P.M.L.A.* 79 (1968), pp. 13-21.

Hotson, Leslie, *Shakespeare's motley (London, 1952)*.

Howkins, Alun, 'Whitsun in nineteenth century Oxfordshire', *History workshop pamphlets*, 8 (Oxford, 1974).

Idler, The, (1759 and 1893).

Irving, Washington, *The sketch book and Bracebridge Hall* (London, 1891).

Jackson, John, *The history of the Scottish stage* (Edinburgh, 1793).

Judge, Roy, *The Jack in the Green* (Ipswich, 1979).

Kennedy, Douglas, *English folk dancing* (London, 1964).

Kingston Churchwardens' account book KG2/2/1.

Kirks, John, *The seven champions of Christendome* (1638).

Knutsford Royal May-day Guides (1934 and 1981).

Lancashire Figaro or the northern charivari, The, (1881).

Lea, Katherine, M. *Italian popular comedy: a study in the* Commedia dell'Arte, *1550-1620, with special reference to the English stage* (Oxford, 1934).

Leach, A.F. *Memorials of Beverley Minster* (Durham, 1898-1903).

Leach, A.F. *Beverley town documents* (London, 1900).

Le Roux, H. and J. Garnier, *Acrobats and mountebanks* (London, 1890).

Lowe, Barbara, 'Early records of the morris in England', *J.E.F.D. & S.S.* 8 (1957), pp. 61-82.

Macaulay, George, *The history of England from the accession of James II* (London, 1858).

Machyn, Henry, *The diary of a resident in London*, J.G. Nicols, ed. (London, 1848).

Manchester Mercury, 18 May 1773.

Marchant, Thomas, *Diary 1714-1728, Sussex archeaological society publications*, vol. 25 (1873).

Mares, F.H. 'The origin of the figure called the Vice', *Huntington Library Quarterly*, 22 (1958) pp. 11-29.

Mask, The (1868).

Mayer, David, *Harlequin in his element* (Harvard University press, 1969).

Mayhew, Henry, *London labour and the London poor* (London,

1851).

Merry Andrews epistle to his old master Benjamin, a mountebank at Bangor-bridge (London, 1719).

Merry Andrew or, the humours of a fair (Shrewsbury, 1820).

Merry-go-round, The, C. Forward, ed. (London, 1894).

Miall, A. and P. *The Victorian Christmas book* (London, 1978).

Miller, James, *The man of taste* (London, 1735).

Mirc, John, *Instructions for parish priests,* E. Peacocke, ed. *E.E.T.S.* (London, 1868).

Monthly magazine (1798), pt. 1.

Morley, Henry, *Memoirs of Bartholomew fair* (London, 1848).

More, St Thomas, *The complete works* (New Haven, 1965).

Nashe, Thomas, *The works of Thomas Nasha,* R.B. McKerrow, ed. (Oxford, 1958).

Nichols, C.W. 'Fielding's satire on pantomime', *P.M.L.A.* vol. 44 (1931) pp. 1107-12.

Nicoll, Allardyce, *The world of Harlequin* (Cambridge, 1963).

Nikolaus von Kues, Werke, P. Wilpert, ed. (Berlin, 1967).

Ordish, T.F. 'Folk-drama', *Folklore,* vol. 2 (1891) pp. 314-35 and vol. 4 (1893) pp. 149-75.

Owen, Trefor, *Welsh folk customs* (Cardiff, 1959).

Palmer, Roy, ed. *Everyman's book of British ballads* (London, 1980).

Paterson, Peter, *Glimpses of real life as seen in the theatrical world* (Edinburgh, 1864).

Paulson, G. *A history of Beverley* (London, 1829).

Peraldus, Guilelmus, *Summa virtutem ac vitiorum* (Moguntiae, 1618).

Pettitt, Thomas, 'Ritual and vaudeville: the dramaturgy of the English folk plays', *Pre-publications of the English Institute of Odense University,* 19 (1981).

Pettitt, Thomas, 'English folk drama in the eighteenth century', *Comparative drama* 1 (1981) vol. 15.

Richards, Raymond, *The Manor of Gawsworth: a history* (Manchester, 1975).

Robertson, D.W. and Huppé, D.F., *Piers Plowman and Scriptural tradition* (London, 1951).

Robson William, *The old play-goer* (London, 1854).

Rollins, H.E. 'The Commonwealth drama: miscellaneous

notes', *S.P.* vol. 20 (1923) pp. 52-69 and 'A contribution to the history of the English Commonwealth', *S.P.* vol. 18 (1921), pp. 267-333.

Roomer and *Transmission*, P. Smith and S. Roud, eds. Centre for English cultural traditions and language, University of Sheffield.

Rosenfeld, Sybil, *The theatre of the London fairs in the eighteenth century* (Cambridge, 1960).

Salopian shreds and patches, vols. 7-9 (Shrewsbury, 1885-7).

Sandler, Lucy Freeman, *The Peterborough Psalter in Brussels and other Fenland manuscripts* (London, 1974).

Sandys, William, *Christmas carols* (London, 1833).

Sandys, William, *Christmastide: its history, festivities and carols* (London, 1852).

Saward, John, 'The fool for Christ's sake in Monasticism East and West', *Theology and Prayer*, vol. 3 (Oxford, 1975).

Scott, C. *The drama of yesterday*, 2 vols. (London, 1899).

Scrap book of literary varieties (London, 1831-2).

Sharp. Cecil, *The morris book* (London, 1912).

Sisson, C.J. *Lost plays of Shakespeare's age* (Cambridge, 1936).

Sleare, Dr *Philosophical Collections*, vol. 3 (1681) pp. 48-50.

Smith, J.T. *Ancient topography of London* (London, 1815).

Smith, J.T. *Vagabondiana* (London, 1817).

Smith, Lucy, T. ed. *The York Mystery Cycle* (London, 1885).

Speaight, George, *Punch and Judy: a history* (London, 1955).

Stow, John, *A survey of London, 1603*, C.L. Kingsford, ed. (Oxford, 1971).

Strutt, Joseph, *Sports and pastimes of the people of England*, William Hone, ed. (London, 1831).

Stubbes, *Anatomie of abuses in the kingdom of Ailgna*, F.J. Furnivall, ed. (London, 1877-82).

Swain, Barbara, *Fools and folly during the middle ages and the Renaissance* (New York, 1932).

Thomas, Tobias, *The life of the late famous comedian, Joseph Hayns* (London, 1701).

Thomas of Chobham *Summa confessorum*, F. Broomfield, ed. *Analecta Mediaevalia Namurcenses* (Paris, 1968).

Thomas, W. *Anecdotes and traditions illustrative of early English history and literature, Camden society publication* (London, 1839).

Thornley, Ida, ed. *The great Chronicle of London* (London, 1938).

Thrupp, John, *The Anglo-Saxon home* (London, 1862).

Tiddy, R.J.E., *The mummers' play* (Oxford, 1923).

Walsh, William, *Curiosities of popular customs and of rites, ceremonies observances, and miscellaneous antiquities* (London, 1898).

Ward, Ned, *The London spy* (1690).

Weaver, John, *The history of the mimes and pantomimes* (London, 1728).

Welsford, Enid, *The court masque* (Cambridge, 1927).

Welsford, Enid, *The fool* (London, 1935).

Wickham, Glynne, *English moral interludes* (London, 1976).

Wildridge, Tindale, *The misericords of Beverley Minster* (Hull, 1879).

Wilkinson, T.T. ed. *Legends and traditions of Lancashire* (Manchester, 1873).

Willeford, William, *The fool and his sceptre* (Northwestern University press, 1969).

Williams, P.V.A. ed. *The fool and the trickster* (Ipswich, 1979).

Wright, A.R. *British calendar customs*, T.E. Lones, ed. *Folklore society publications* (London, 1936-7).

Yonge, C.M. *The Christmas mummers* (London, 1858).

Appendix

A chronological list of Fool illustrations in English manuscripts.

THIRTEENTH CENTURY

Trin. Coll. Camb. MSB. 11.5. *Psalter* (Anglo-Norman) 1173-1220: fol. 73r.

Bodl. MS Gough Liturg. 2. *Missal circa* 1300: fol. 221v.

New Coll. Oxford MS 7. *Bible* 1220-1230. fol. 142r.

Bodl. MS Auct. D.4.6.: *Psalter* 1158-64: fol. 96v.

Bodl. MS Rawl. G.23: *Psalter* 1265-70: fol. 57r.

All Souls Coll. Oxford MS 2: *Bible* 1250-75: fol. 180r.

Bodl. MS. Auct. D.5.9.: *Bible* 1250-1300: fol. 289v.

New Coll. Oxford MS 1: *Bible* 1270-1300: fol. 185v.

Bodl. MS Canon Bibl. Lat. 11: *Bible* 1250-70: fol. 238v.

Trin. Coll. Camb. MS 0.4.27: *Bible* 1280-1300: fol. 231v.

Camb. MS Dd 15.17 (H): *Psalter* 1280-1300: fol. 72v.

Nat. Lib. of Scotland MS 1.1.1: *Ruskin Bible* 1250-1300: fol. 208r.

BM MS Add. 21,926: *Psalter* 1280-1300: fol. 82r.

Bodl. MS Rawl. G.126: *Psalter circa* 1300: fol. 221v.

Fitzwilliam Mus. Camb. MS 2: *Bible circa* 1300: Fol. 207v.

Camb. MS Add. 4090: *Psalter circa* 1300: fol. 82r.

Fitzwilliam Mus. Camb. McLean Coll. MS 13: *Bible* 1200-1300: fol. 257r.

Bodl. MS Auct. D. inf. 2.2: *Bible* 1275-1300: fol. 60r.

Exeter Coll. Oxford, MS 42: *Etymology circa* 1300: fol. 12r.

Bibliotheque Royale, Brussels MS 9961-62: *Peterborough Psalter circa* 1300: fol. 41r.

BM MS Royal 2.B.7: *Queen Mary Psalter circa* 1300: fol. 150v.

Merton Coll. Oxford MS H.2.2: *Bible circa* 1300: fol. 191r.

FOURTEENTH CENTURY

Corpus Christi Coll. Oxford MS 98: *Codex* 1300-1310: fol. 45r.

Bodl. Liturg. 198: *Psalter* 1300-1400: fol. 47r.

Pierpoint Morgan Library, New York, MS M.302: *Ramsay Psalter* 1300-20: fol. 64r.

Bodl. MS Barlow 22: *Barlow Psalter* 1300-30: fols. 67 and 68r.

Bodl. MS Douce b.4: MS clippings fol. 4a.

Pierpoint Morgan Library, MS M.102: *The Windmill Psalter* 1300-20.*

Corpus Christi Coll. Camb. Parker MS 53: *The Stukeley Psalter* 1300-20: fol. 64r.

Merton Coll. Oxford 0.2.5: *Analytics* (Kilwardy & Grosseteste) 1300-1400: fol. 148r.

Bodl. MS Douce 366: *Ormesby Psalter* 1300-1350: fol. 72r.

Bodl. MS Astor A.1: *Hours of the Virgin c* 1350: fol. 91v.

Jesus Coll. Oxford MS.D.40: *Psalter* 1300-1400: fol. 71v.

Pierpoint Morgan Library MS G.53: *Psalter of Richard of Canterbury* 1300-20*

BM MS Arun. 83.1: *Howard Psalter* 1300-30.*

Bodl. MS Ashmole 1523: *Bromholm Psalter* 1300-40: fol. 66r.

BM MS Stowe 12: *Breviary* 1322-25: fol. 180v.

BM MS Add. 39810: *St Omer Psalter* 1300-40: fol. 57v.

Bodl. MS Douce 131: *Psalter* 1300-40: fol. 43r.

BM MS Add. 42130: *Luttrell Psalter* 1300-40: fol. .98v.

All Souls Coll. Oxford MS 7: *Psalter* 1300-40: fol. 49v.

Lambeth Palace Library MS 233: *Psalter* 1300-40: fol. 82v.

Sidney Sussex Coll. Camb. MS 76: *Psalter* 1300-40: fol. 47r.

Camb. MS Mm.5.36(E): *Psalter* 1300-30: fol. 65r.

Camb. MS D.d.5: *Countess of Pembroke's Breviary c* 1340: fol. 28v.

Camb. MS Add. 4500(G): *Breviary* 1300-1400: fol. 294v.

BM MS Royal 1.E.9: *The Richard IInd Bible c* 1380: fol. 148r.

Bodl. MS Auct. D.2.2.: *Canterbury Psalter* c 1320: fol. 60r.

Bodl. MS Rawl. G.185: *Psalter from Dublin* 1300-1400: fol. 43v.

Bodl. Ms Kennicott 15: *Bible* 1300-1400: fol. 120r.

Bodl. MS Auct. D.3.5: *Bible* 1300-1400: fol. 120r.

Bodl. MS Gough Liturg. 8: *Psalter* 1300-1400: fol. 27r.

Bodl. MS Douce 211: *Psalter* 1300-1400: fol. 258v.

Longleat, Marquiss of Bath: *Longleat Psalter*: 1300-30.*

Dr. William's Library, London MS Anc.6: Psalter 1300-30.*
Douai Biblioteque Publique MS 171: *Psalter* 1300-40.*
Corpus Christi Coll. Oxford MS E.18: *Psalter* c 1390: fol. 44v.

FIFTEENTH CENTURY

Corpus Christi Coll. Oxford MS 17: *Psalter* c 1400: fol. 55r.
Bodl. Ms Bodley 953: *Berkeley Breviary* c 1400: page 173.
Bodl. MS Gough Liturg. 18: *Psalter c* 1400: fol. 55r.
Brasenose Coll. Oxford MS F.16: *Psalter* c 1420: fol. 70v.
Bodl. MS Land. Lat. 114 : *Psalter* 1400-1500 : fol, 71r.
Bodl. MS Douce 18: *Psalter* 1433-62: fol. 113v.
New York Public Library, Spenser Collection, MS 3: *The Wing-field Psalter* 1450: fol. 38r.
Trin. Coll. Camb. MS 0.3.10: *Psalter* 1400-1450: fol. 44r.
BM MS Royal 2.A.12: *Breviary c* 1490: fol. 304r.
Bodl. MS Liturg. 153: *Psalter c* 1420: fol. 49v.
Bodl. MS Hatton 10: *Statutes of England to 1495:* fol. 43r.

* See L.F. Sandler

Index